ALL ABOARD THE GRACIE TRAIN

ALL ABOARD THE GRACIE TRAIN

GARY SAVAGE

ALL ABOARD THE GRACE TRAIN

A Jiu-Jitsu Journey

ALL ABOARD THE GRACIE TRAIN

Published by

Savage Publishing

Copyright © 2021 Gary Savage

The author asserts their moral right to be identified as the author of this book.

First published in Great Britain in 2021.

ISBN: 9798789363713

All rights reserved. No part of this book may be reproduced in any written, electronic, recording, or photocopying without written permission of the publisher or authors, except as permitted by the UK Copyright, Designs and Patents Act 1988, without the prior permission of the publisher.

Although every precaution has been taken to verify the accuracy of the information contained herein, the author and publisher assume no responsibility for any errors or omissions. No liability is assumed for damages that may result from the use of information contained within.

This book is sold subject to the condition that it shall not, by way of trade or otherwise, be lent, resold, hired out, or otherwise circulated without the publisher's prior consent in any form of binding or cover other than that in which it is published and without a similar condition including this condition being imposed on the subsequent publisher.

Cover design by Gary Savage

Edited by Gemma Scott

Dedication

Dedicated to the headmasters, Carlos and Hélio Gracie, and all that graduated from the old school. Some still with us, some sadly not. Those stubborn few that dared to question, to seek and ultimately find. They reached for the stars. They believed in a dream. They laid the foundations, they walked a lonely road and in so doing gave us the ultimate gift that keeps on giving, *Brazilian Jiu-Jitsu*. Now is our time to carry the torch, to keep the flame burning, to lead the way for the next generation.

'I created a flag from the sport's dignity. I oversee the name of my family with affection, steady nerves and blood' - Hélio Gracie.

Table of Contents

Introduction *11*

   In the beginning there was Chuck! 11

Chapter 1 .... *13*

   'You can't fight sleep' 13

Chapter 2 .... *15*

   But I won't do that! 15

Chapter 3 .... *21*

   Train Spotting 21

Chapter 4 .... *27*

   You Say Jiu-Jitsu, I say Jujitsu 27

Chapter 5 .... *33*

   The Tale of The Tape 33

Chapter 6 .... *38*

   Rolls, Royce, and the Ultimate Gracie Machine 38

Chapter 7 .... *40*

   The Emperor's New Clothes 40

Chapter 8 .... *42*

   The Changing of the (old) Guard 42

Chapter 9 .... *44*

   The Lion, the switch and the wardrobe (malfunction) 44

Chapter 10 .... *47*

   If we build it, they will come! 47

Chapter 11 .... *53*

    The Lone Shark! 53

Chapter 12 59
    God speaks and I listen 59

Chapter 13 66
    A storm in a sports cup 66

Chapter 14 75
    Still All White on the Night 75

Chapter 15 78
    Who's afraid of the Big Bad Wolf! 78

Chapter 16 82
    Blue is the colour-Jiu-Jitsu is the game 82

Chapter 17 88
    Roll Call 88

Chapter 18 92
    Purple Reign 92

Chapter 19 98
    Nirvana 98

Chapter 20 105
    Brief Encounter 105

Chapter 21 110
    Theatre of Dreams 110

Chapter 22 115
    It's All in Your Mind 115

Chapter 23 120
    Walk the line 120

Chapter 24 126

Black and Blue	126
Chapter 25	*130*
A Ticket to Ride	130
Chapter 26	*133*
End of the Line or New Destination?	133
Chapter 27	*135*
Standing on the Shoulders of Giants	135
Epilogue	*137*
Run Over by a Train	137

Introduction

In the beginning there was Chuck!

The Gracie family are to Jiu-Jitsu and the development of modern-day martial arts, what Sir Isaac Newton was to Gravity. In short, this family of Brazilian bad asses revolutionized the way we train, fight and view systems of hand-to-hand combat that have been around long before the Granny Smith's apple parted Sir Isaac's hair.

The Gracie version of the 'What Goes Up Must Come Down' theory seems to have taken a tad longer than Newton's apple falling on the head, lightbulb moment. Carlos and Hélio Gracie had started their thesis in 1926, but prior to the Ultimate Fighting Challenge 1, only a select few had heard of the Gracie family outside of their native Brazil.

In the USA, Chuck Norris (of course) and one or two lesser mortals *(the rest of the planet falling into that category compared to Chuck)*, had recognised the importance of the Gospel that Hélio and his family were spreading and had decided to see what all the fuss was about. However, it wasn't until the eldest son Rorian Gracie teamed up with an American entrepreneur, Art Davy, to develop a format to showcase the effectiveness of the family art (which became The Ultimate Fighting Challenge), that the rest of the (more enlightened) martial arts community jumped onto what was to become a runaway bandwagon.

I was in one of the groups we will refer to as AC (after Chuck). I became obsessed with all things Gracie Jiu-Jitsu (GJJ), however there was one problem, there were hardly any Gracie Jiu-Jitsu schools outside of Brazil - or America for that matter. This wouldn't be such an insurmountable problem if I lived in either of these countries, but I didn't. No, ladies and gentlemen, I was blessed with being an Englishman, the nation that a giant can smell the blood of from 500 paces. A people depicted in Hollywood films as the 'jolly hockey stick,' cut-glass accented stereotypes that say, 'hard cheese' and wear Bowler hats, or alternatively to be found dancing in the streets of our capital city singing *'who will buy my strawberries?'* Worse still, and to add to my frustration, I was a Northerner. Stereotyped by the Bowler hatted 'hard cheese' brigade as a flat cap wearing pigeon fancier. 'Strong int arm, thick int ead'. Anyway, as it came to pass it didn't make much of a difference which side of the Watford gap you were born on, it was to be a long and frustrating wait before Gracie, or as it was to be collectively known, *Brazilian Jiu-Jitsu* (BJJ) would touch down on British soil.

This is the story of Brazilian jiu-jitsu in the UK. A Jiu-Jitsu journey that I invite you to take with me. It starts and ends with the Gracie family, but it goes beyond their remarkable influence. We will make regular stops on our day trip along the evolutionary track, and I will attempt to be your tour guide. I can only narrate as it happened to me. But I am sure that you will see some common threads running through the story.

Jujitsu is an ever-changing art and dinosaurs like me have had to move with the times in order to dodge the extinction bullet. We can't fight change, it is inevitable and, in many respects, necessary to survival. This great art, the *Arte Suave*, the gentle art, has done more than survive, it has prospered beyond our wildest dreams.

This book is a celebration of change rather than a resistance to change. It isn't a *'things were better in the good old days'* message, although it nods to a time that in some respects had its moments and were indeed 'good days'.

The story is 28 years in the making (at the time of writing this book in 2021). And what a story it is. Sometimes funny, other times sad, but always (hopefully) entertaining. And it doesn't matter if you were standing on the platform in 1993 or caught the train a bit later, there will be something that resonates in you, I promise. So, grab a British Rail cheese and ham toastie and a beverage of your choice and get on board the 'Gracie Train'.

'A story is like a moving train: no matter where you hop onboard, you are bound to reach your destination sooner or later.' Khaled Hosseini

Chapter 1

'You can't fight sleep'

'The Midnight Express'

Present Day, Northern England.

I wake (or rather I am awoken) from a deep slumber, a cursory glance at the clock tells me it's 11.30pm. My first thought, *who the fuck is calling me at this time of night?* The number displayed is not recognised as one of my contacts. I lift the phone to my mangled left ear.

- 'Hello'

- 'Hey man, is that the fighting gym?'

- 'It is the mixed martial arts gym yes, how can I help you?'

- 'Sweet. I want to do UFC.'

- *'(Sighs) UFC is an organisation not a fighting style.'*

- 'No, I want to do that Conor McGregor stuff, you know, UFC.'

- 'You are not listening to me. The UFC is an organisation that stages mixed martial arts competitions, there is no fighting style called UFC, I teach Brazilian jiu-jitsu and mixed martial arts.'

- 'Yeah, that sounds ok. What's Jiu-Jitsu, isn't that all the pyjama fighting stuff?'

   '(Sighs) Have you ever heard of the Gracies?'

- 'No mate who is she?'

- *'(Sighs) Never mind.'*

- 'Can you get me a UFC fight or not?'

- 'I think you have more chance of getting a fight in KFC, I can help you with that!'

I end the call, having given out my gym address and advising the wannabe Conor Mac as to my business hours. I know in all likelihood I'll never see him. It feels like I have sold my soul to the Devil.

I close my eyes again. But sleep won't come. My mind takes me back. Back to the start. Or at least a start.

Chapter 2

But I won't do that!
'Full Steam Ahead'

November 12th, 1993, Northern England.

Something was wrong. I could feel it. It didn't feel like a Friday. Usually by this time of the week I would be bouncing around like an energetic puppy, excited by the prospect of a reprise from the factory floor.

Today, I was reflective, reserved, almost to the point of being sullen. Even the usual workplace banter that bordered on the 'gone too far' spectrum floated effortlessly above my head. The factory radio speakers strained as Meat Loaf told us how he *'would do anything for love, but I won't do that'*. I contemplated just what it was that he wasn't prepared to do. Had his significant other rocked up in a rubber catsuit complete with gimp mask, a whip and a can of squirty cream? No, that would be far too tame for someone that answered to Meat Loaf rather than his given birth name. It must be something really weird, rockstars don't seem the type to blush easily, they are not renowned for being prudes. Maybe she had asked him to sort out his sock draw or get rid of that handkerchief he insisted on carrying everywhere (he doesn't even look like he has a cold).

My mind shifted direction. Was it Meat, Mr. Loaf or just plain Meat Loaf if introduced I mused. Not that there was much chance of bumping into Mr. Loaf anytime soon, he wasn't a regular in the Railway Tavern.

My train of thought was derailed as Sicknote, so called because, well you get the gist, shouted *'oi Sav, you going to the Railway with your boyfriend tonight?'* Hilarious. Sicknote never missed an opportunity to showcase his witty repartee. *'Sorry mate I presumed it was a geezer I saw you with last Saturday as it was far too ugly to be a bird'* he continued. And there you had it. Now usually I would pick Sicknote up, come back with a sharp response that would no doubt confuse, but have the desired effect of putting him firmly in his place. Only today, I feigned a smile that disguised my inner contempt for the pale, skinny, work-shy little fob that now stood before me, shoulders heaving as he laughed at his well-rehearsed and over-egged gag. He disarmed me somewhat as he continued, *'It is my birthday* after all. Few drinks in town or what?' 'Yeah ok', I heard my reply long before my brain had time to engage.

Later that evening I stared into a lukewarm pint of lager as if searching a crystal ball for a clue to explain my flat mood (I had long since given up on the Meat Loaf quandary). I examined the evidence like Holmes, Poirot or Marple might.

Ok, so I had turned 30 earlier this month. *Tick.*

I worked in a dead-end job that had no real prospects, other than the risk of losing my mind, dignity and maybe my liberty (if I snapped and put Sicknote out of his misery). *Tick.*

I was in and out of relationships with a depressing regularity (my mother had even given up asking *'when are you going to settle down'*). *Tick.*

I lived in a flat that I could hardly afford to heat (I had taken to wearing most of my clothes in an attempt to stay alive during the coldest of winter evenings). *Tick.*

In short, I came to a beer-hazed conclusion that had the Railway Tavern announced the world's biggest loser competition that very evening (first prize, a stein of lager), I was a shoe in to win, which is something of a paradox. Winning a biggest loser contest - and that was saying something in this bar.

As I scanned the horizon, my eyes were drawn to Sicknote, swaying like a man on a tightrope, arms extended, beer spilling from his glass as he delivered his best chat up lines to Big Julie, AKA 'Martini' (any time, any place, anywhere). She was what you might describe as a 'homely girl' (if your home was Fraggle Rock), attractive in a hard looking way, with piercing blue eyes. She let herself down when she spoke and the sort of narrative that you might expect from a squaddie came spewing forth from a mouth which housed a grill that resembled a row of burnt chips.

Sicknote certainly had his birthday beer goggles on. This could lift my mood, if only temporarily. I was already going over my wind ups for Monday mornings' matinee performance at work. Suddenly, my life didn't quite seem as hopeless.

It got a whole lot rosier as Big Jules grabbed my now helpless work colleague by the scruff of the neck and pulled him in for a long and somewhat sloppy exchange of saliva. The only thing missing from this scene, which my fertile imagination was quick to provide, was the voice-over of David Attenborough narrating the scene...

'Here we see the lesser spotted Sicknote has wandered into the wrong area. Separated from the herd, he is in unimaginable danger. A predator is lying in wait. She blends in effortlessly with her surroundings, ready to make her move. And there it is, nature at its most basic yet brutal. The weak and disorientated Sicknote becomes tonight's main course, all washed down with a G and T. He puts up a valiant last ditch bid for freedom before succumbing to his fate. And the circle of life continues.'

My last sighting of Sicknote on that particular evening was of him being (fireman) carried out of the bar by Big Julie as a group of the collective birthday entourage formed a conga behind. My eyes met the now bloodshot eyes of Sicknote for the briefest of moments and I am sure that I saw him mouth *'help me'* as he disappeared from view. I was brave, but not brave enough to get in the way of true love. *'Happy birthday old chum'* I said, raising my warm beer as the last of the line-up kicked their left leg out in perfect unison with the human train that went ahead.

I woke the next day in a better mood, albeit it with a headache, and on the floor surrounded with empty beer bottles and half eaten pizza slices. It was my Jujitsu class in a couple of hours. Time for the hangover to subside.

'There's a guy works down the chip shop, swears he's Elvis!'

I loved my martial arts, always had. It was the only thing I had ever really shown any aptitude for. My dad had started a spark by showing me some of his 'unarmed combat' moves as a child. Bruce Lee had poured petrol onto the spark, which now raged like an uncontrollable forest fire within. I had dabbled in several martial arts, from Karate to Judo, before deciding that Japanese Jujitsu was the most practical for self-defence. I was 85% certain that I was training in the right martial art. However, and this was always a problem for me, I wasn't prepared to take the art at face value, I had to test it. I could get into a fight in an empty room, so researching Jujitsu's practicality wasn't a problem. What was a problem was the number of times I was waking up in a police cell!

I wanted to hone my skills, to be unbeatable, but this came at a cost. I knew that real fights were messy. They lacked the almost dance like aesthetic that was displayed in the Dojo. I also knew that a complete system of combat had to be practical and adaptable in any range.

I chose Jujitsu as my base martial art when a few years earlier myself and a good friend Chris, found ourselves in a particularly hairy situation outside a less than salubrious public house. We had been watching our friend play guitar and sing in a working men's club, and during a break in proceedings decided to venture into this new (to us) watering hole.

It was like a scene from *American Werewolf in London*, the part where the two ramblers walk into the pub on the moors. Everything seemed to stop as we pushed open the door. All eyes, or so it seemed, were burning into us. Chris wasn't fazed. We ordered a couple of beers and sat in a corner, taking in our new surroundings.

'What the fuck are you looking at?' came a voice from the bar. This bloke was straight out of *Westside Story*. His hair was greased in a 'DA style'. He looked like the love child of Elvis Presley and Ted from *Hi-de-Hi!* He obviously thought he looked cool in his t-shirt with a pack of fags rolled up the sleeve, skin-tight black jeans and the 'look', if you could call it that, finished off with a pair of brothel creepers.

To me he looked like the prick that he obviously was. Chris smiled and said, *'fuck knows'*, or words to that effect. This enraged the tin pot Danny Zuko so much that he put his pint down and said *'outside, now'*. Chris was happy to oblige.

I had known Chris for a few months, and we had gotten in a fair few scrapes during this time, I knew he could handle himself but seeing Elvis the pelvis and several of the T-Birds head for the door, I knew we were outnumbered and in all likelihood in for a beating.

The gang surrounded us. I was weighing up which one to chin first when Chris put his hands up in an almost apologetic way. *'Listen mate'*, he said to Elvis, *'there's no need for everyone to get involved, just me and you.'* Elvis seemed confused. He certainly wasn't MENSA material, but even this most simple of statements seemed to flummox him.

What happened next took me and the circling goons by surprise. Chris didn't wait for a response, he hit him with a ridge hand, looped his arm around his neck and performed a very efficient outer reaping throw that saw our Greasy friend making a rather fast acquaintance with the cold hard pavement.

It's fair to say that he went down so hard that it's a wonder his body print isn't still there. Elvis had left the building and was now sleeping like a baby.

Chris turned to the rest of the gang and said, *'right who's next?'* Surprisingly, the rest of the wild bunch didn't want to avenge their fallen leader, instead muttering apologies before dragging his prone body back towards the pub.

Anyway, Chris had done some Jujitsu or unarmed combat in the army, and it had certainly served us well that night. Jujitsu it was then.

My drive to the gym later that day saw me contemplating last night's events. Not just Sicknote's hilarious fate (although it still made me chuckle every time I conjured up the image of his skinny limp frame bouncing atop Big Jules shoulders). No, there was a deeper feeling, an unshakable thought that yesterday something momentous had occurred and I, as is often the case, had missed it.

It was bizarre as the news headlines didn't offer any clue as to what it was that I felt an overwhelming fear of missing out on. Oh well, no point dwelling on things that were only a feeling, this was 1993 after all, what a time to be alive, technology was at its absolute peak, I mean who would have thought you could make a phone call from a device that had no wires and was usable anywhere (within reason) and even better it looked so cool, just like those walkie talkies the army used. Heady times indeed, what will they think of next? I needed to get me one of those, but for now I was feeling like the dogs every time I opened my Filofax. So what if the only information I had in it was my hairdressers' number (I had to keep the Kevin Keegan perm looking fly) and a couple of lady's phone numbers, including, I noticed, Big Jules. I can't remember writing that in or why I had it (honestly M'Lud).

My Jujitsu class went surprisingly well, given that my hangover had repapered just like an axe wielding maniac in a bad horror film (just when you think they are dead, they rise one last time and try to bury that hatchet into the heroine's head, before finally succumbing to another bullet).

It would be a few years later that the mysterious feeling of missing out on some life changing event would make sense and I could join the dots. November 12th, 1993, it turned out was a special day, a momentous day, a day that would change my life forever. I just didn't realise it at the time, I didn't realise it until 2 years later when someone at the gym handed me a bootleg copy of a video and said, 'watch this, it's fucking mental'.

*November 12th, 1993 didn't just change MY life. Some 9 months after their eyes met across the Railway Tavern bar, Sicknote and Big Julie welcomed their first-born, Chardonnay, into the world. And unlike Mr. Loaf, Sicknote, it appears, was prepared to do anything for love, including 'that'.

Chapter 3

Train Spotting

'Train arrive'

Ultimate Fighting Challenge 1 - November 12th, 1993, Denver Colorado, USA

The camera panned through a crowd dense with sweaty, drunk, lumberjack shirt wearing, all American daydream believers. Miller Lite beer cans raised triumphantly aloft mullet cuts (the uniform coiffure of this restless throng), all calling, as if one, for their pound of flesh. If nothing else these men and some women, but mainly men, liked their violence violent, and their entertainment big, ballsy and brash. Tonight, they would not be disappointed.

The battle arena was unlike anything I had ever seen, an 8-sided chain fenced cage - an Octagon. Once in, you were in, until you were out, either as a result of concussion or some other brutal and honest end to the fight.

To a layperson, used to watching his hand-to-hand combat in a ring, with rules, this was bordering on the barbaric. This was no Madison Square Garden all singing, all dancing affair. For one, it wasn't boxing, or for that matter wrestling. It was, or so the commentators had tried to explain, a contest to determine the best and most effective martial art. It looked like an underground fight club, or at least what I imagined an underground fight club to look like (this was some time before Brad Pitt gave us the first rule).

I hadn't taken my eyes off of the scene as it unfolded on the grainy VHS copy, I had tentatively loaded into the video player earlier that night. It was the early part of the 1990's and long before Blu-ray, streaming or even YouTube had revolutionised the way we viewed, learned and studied. And, although I was watching this 'new' concept in combat sport, fought and filmed in Denver Colorado, in the good old US of A, back home in the good old North of England, it felt like a strange throwback to days long gone. A time I had only read about or seen in historically inaccurate Hollywood movies like Ben-Hur, a time when gladiators fought for their life rather than reputation. This was *'The Ultimate*

Fighting Challenge (UFC)', martial artist vs martial artist; *mano a mano*. A chance to prove who had the best kick ass moves.

For centuries man had debated who was the 'daddy', the Karate guy with his high kicking prowess and board breaking skill, or the wrestler with the ability to tie a man in knots. This was the King Kong vs Godzilla battle to end all battles of the martial art universe. The wait was nearly over. We were about to find out once and for all who, or rather what was the best fighting method.

If I had thought that the unfolding spectacle was in the same vein as the theatrical and much worked pantomime wrestling bouts that graced the British television screens in the 70's and 80's, then I was about to get a wake up and smell the coffee moment that would stay with me long after the initial caffeine kick had worn off. This was no Big Daddy vs Giant Haystacks Saturday afternoon belly battle. There were no raging blue rinse grannies eager to part the hair with their lethal handbag accuracy of the fall guy wrestler that employed dubious methods to solicit the cry of 'uncle' against their favourite spandex wearing grappling Demi God.

The night had started with a bout between a kickboxer and a sumo wrestler, what's not to love. There were no rules apparently and anything was allowed, other than eye-gouging or fish-hooking (pulling someone's mouth open). This was to be a short and not so sweet affair when the tall and pale kickboxer, Gerard, dropped the sumo guy and hoofed him so hard in the face that one of his teeth took flight and ended up in row 5 aisle C. No doubt destined to be retrieved and worn as a souvenir on a string tie by one of the more discerning patrons. Oh, how we love a souvenir.

The sumo wrestler protested the loss (not the tooth), after the referee had intervened and stopped the fight. I must admit it seemed a bit odd that the outcome was decided due to a molar being dislodged. It's not as if the huge Hawaiian sumo wrestler was KO'd. Plus, he had plenty of other teeth left to tear to shreds the mountains of food required to keep his impressive athletic shape. It mattered not, the fight was over, and the crowd was satiated, they had tasted first blood (literally, if seated in the front row).

The commentator tried desperately to build some excitement for the next bout. This turned out to be a slugfest between an overweight kickboxer who wore his shorts on the high side (think early Simon Cowell) and a man in better physical shape who at least wore his fighting apparel at a level that didn't make him look like he was wearing a nappy.

This fight lasted longer than the first, even if it resembled a drunken brawl between two middle aged men at a wedding. So far there wasn't much evidence of any martial art technique, just John Wayne-esque slugging or as our American friends say 'swinging for the fences'.

The larger of the two, Kevin (high shorts), survived an early onslaught of knuckle shattering punches (did I mention they wore no gloves?) to eventually turn the tide against his exhausted opponent. A couple of stomps to the head sealed the victory and catapulted Kevin into the semi-finals along with Gerard and his unfortunate and slightly concussed opponent enroute to the local A and E department.

A Horse Named Gracie?

The music swelled from synthesizer to power chord crescendo. Laser lighting bounced in time, caught in a heavy and dense, fog-filled air. Fight number 3 was about to get under way.

I must say that at this point I was marginally disappointed with the event. After all, it was hardly Enter the Dragon. I could have gone into town on any given Saturday night and watched people, some of whom, incidentally, who had a penchant for wearing their trousers under their armpits, slugging each other and leaving dance floors stained with blood and littered with teeth.

I decided (wisely with hindsight) to give the video a bit longer before I replaced it with a bootleg copy of Jurassic Park. It wasn't really a hard decision as an earlier and brief look at Spielberg's dinosaur movie showed that the quality was so bad that the T-Rex made Barney look more threatening. Anyway, on with the show.

The human carriage made up of brothers, uncles and sons, their hands resting on the shoulders of the man in front, cut its path, unknowingly taking one small step for man, one giant leap for martial kind as it went.

A young boy, no more than 14 years old, led the tracksuit wearing, clean cut and deeply tanned ensemble with an air of assuredness, giving the spectacle an even more darkly comedic sense of the absurd. But it was the man at the centre of the pack that demanded attention, and not just because he was the only one dressed in the battle fatigues of the martial artist, a white Gi, tied at the waist with the much-coveted black belt. There was something else that shifted the gaze from the baying crowd and the obvious side-show of family unity. The chosen one, head bowed, lightly touching the back of his brother, his steps fast but shallow as he was led towards what looked like the modern-day equivalent of an amphitheatre, already stained with the drying blood of those that had gone before. He looked for all the world like a man walking the 'Green Mile', the death row shuffle.

When he eventually raised his head there was a revelation of a boyish, almost innocent and brooding moodiness, like a teenager separated as punishment from his beloved PlayStation. This was not the face of a fighter, or at least what you imagined a fighter to look like. Skinny, almost to the point of being sand kicked in the face puny. The polar opposite of his fellow combatants. God help him. This was starting to feel uncomfortable, like looking at the aftermath of a car crash, as much as you wanted to look away, you couldn't.

As the colourful commentator struggled to add colour to, or even understand the event, the train pulled up and the Gi wearing youth took his place in the centre of the octagon shaped cage. His opponent, a boxer wearing only one glove, looked bemused by the circus and even more so at the task that lay ahead.

At this point I couldn't blame the commentary team or the one gloved boxer for their confusion, I had no clue as to what the hell this was all about either, or for that matter why a man that used his hands as his stock in trade would choose to wear only one boxing glove? The Brazilian was called Royce Gracie, but to further confuse, the R was pronounced as an H, Hoyce Gracie (I misheard and thought he was called Horse Gracie). His stare was as intense as anything I had ever seen. If he was trying to piss off the boxer, he was making a good fist of it (excuse the pun).

And then it happened, the fight was on like Donkey Kong. Shit just got real. Royce Gracie, the rather sulky looking representative from a long and rich dynasty of fighters (so we were reliably informed), just mauled a boxer wearing one glove, with the relative ease of an adult taking candy from a baby (a baby wearing one boxing glove). It happened so fast, I had to rewind the tape and watch it again. And again. And after I realised that this was real and this skinny Brazilian had just dismantled his opponent without breaking a sweat or taking any punishment, I watched it again.

Royce went on to defeat every single one of his opponents in the same easy-like-Sunday-morning manner to be crowned the first Ultimate Fighting Champion. His delight at winning was evident as he told the heckling and booing crowd that he was going 'to Disneyland' to spend his winnings. Forget meeting Mickey and the gang, this was better than finding the golden ticket to Willy Wonka's chocolate factory. Even if the mullet heavy throng had failed to see the genius that was unfolding before their very eyes, I had not.

I was totally sucked in by the whole thing, to say I was impressed was an understatement. It felt like I had been taught the lost chord, shown the promised land, even better, been given a Blue Peter badge. Gracie Jiu-Jitsu had touched down on planet Earth. Now take me to your leader.

This felt much like the 1970's when I had become obsessed with everything Bruce Lee. I had spent a misspent youth chasing the dragon (not the drug), desperate to learn everything about the man and the myth.

There were some similarities, Lee had revolutionised the martial arts world with his cinematic genius and martial mastery, sending everyone Kung Fu crazy. His legend had stood the test of time and his influence never waned in me.

In contrast, Royce Gracie and his family's interpretation of Jujitsu had now shook the traditional systems and buried thousands of years of mysticism in one night, and as Lee had done two decades before, revolutionised martial arts.

There was no death blow greater than that dealt to the traditional arts on that cold November night in 1993. With Gracie's impressive dominance, the idea that Karate, Kung Fu and other long-established systems were unbeatable, was hit with a blow so hard that it needed a standing 8 count. And much like the first time I saw Lee and wanted to learn how to kick the crap out of 10 baddies without breaking a sweat, Gracie's triumph at UFC1 had not only lit a flame in me but threatened to burn me to a crisp.

In short, I wanted to choke people out whilst looking cool in the process, just like Royce. I decided then and there that I would be a BJJ black belt and further that I would meet and train with the first family of BJJ one day. If only I'd realised back then how difficult it would actually be to achieve my goal, I might have had a radical re-think and took an easier option, maybe become an astronaut or learn to split the atom.

Chapter 4

You Say Jiu-Jitsu, I say Jujitsu

'Tickets please'

1995 (ish)

So, there you had it. On the very same night that I had been looking for answers in the bottom of a glass as to my somewhat unfulfilled life, Royce Gracie had made martial arts history. Our sliding door moment saw one of us waking up the morning after covered in glory and adulation, and the other covered in tomato sauce from the previous night's pizza (still stuck to his face). Can you guess which was which?

As stated, this tenuous connection (ok so there really isn't a connection) didn't become apparent until a year or so later when someone at the Jujitsu club handed me a VHS copy that had the words "Ultimate Fighting Challenge 1, November 12th, 1993" scrawled in marker pen across the spine. *'I'll give it a look later'* I said as I threw it into my bag, atop my bloodstained sweaty Gi.

At the time of watching Royce's great moment on the pirate VHS copy, I held a black belt in Japanese Jujitsu, a system that had served samurai warriors well, back in the days of heavy armour and big sharp and pointy swords that is. I was even teaching at a satellite school several days a week.

My introduction to the UFC came at a time when I was (again) questioning my arts practicality. We didn't come across many samurai warriors where I lived. Although I did hear a tale of an aggrieved husband that had found out his best mate had been making extracurricular visits to his missus and decided to even the score with a replica Japanese sword after imbibing a shed load of Stella Artois.

Things didn't quite go to plan for the wannabe Musashi (legendary ronin) and along with his dignity and his wife, he also lost the tip of his big toe after he swung the sword with all skill of... well, a pissed-up forklift driver that had never used a sword in his life (up to that point). It could have been worse; it could have been the tip of something else he detached.

Anyway, on with the story. I was heavily influenced by Bruce Lee, and his philosophical waxing about the 'classical mess' resonated deeply within. I enjoyed training, most of the time, but I was a realist, and knew that some of the techniques although pretty, had little chance of working against a non- compliant person (unless he was wearing heavy samurai armour). I knew because I had tried them in live situations, I had the bruises and the ripped t-shirt to prove it. (P.S. I was not the guilty party in the aforementioned story of the jealous husband and his less than impressive swordsmanship.)

Watching Royce Gracie making classical martial artists look like drunken, barroom brawlers, whilst barely breaking a sweat seemed like the answer to my prayers. He was a Jujitsu guy, just like me, although, I noticed he used the term, Gracie Jiu-Jitsu. And then there was the spelling, Jiu-Jitsu.

'Jujitsu' was my art and therefore the art I was rooting for from the moment the dodgy intro music and visuals started. It didn't register that Royce's Jiu-Jitsu looked nothing like mine. Jujitsu is Jiu-Jitsu by any other name, right? Wrong. After Royce took the one gloved boxer to the canvas, mounted him and solicited a tap out, I was confused as to what had caused the boxer to give up.

By Royce's second outing, things seemed a bit clearer. Again, the Gracie Family had arrived at the cage in style. Only this time the opponent actually looked like he might derail the Gracie train.

Ken Shamrock stood at 6 feet of pure muscle. His chiselled chin and mullet cut made him the poster boy for this ultimate fighting malarkey. We were told that Mr Shamrock was a shoot fighter. I had no clue what that was but couldn't imagine it a very fair fight if he pulled out a Colt 45 and blew Royce's brains out just for some redneck's entertainment.

Turns out that shoot fighting is a wrestling style that is practiced in Japan. And the guy with the mullet is pretty good at it. Royce was going to have his work cut out with Mr Shamrock.

Shamefully, looking back, it was this fight that changed my initial impression that this 'spectacle' was nothing more than a 'martial freakshow'. The previous fights had failed to showcase anything that would make me change that view.

Now seeing through the eyes of a less martially bigoted man, I believe that all of the combatants of that first contest were founding fathers, pioneers, the men that dared to 'go over the top', to sail unchartered waters.

Gracie vs Shamrock shone light on a darkness that I didn't even realise had enveloped me. I had been blinded by the same mysticism that every other martial artist had, back in the days of ignorance. I was a fantasist, wanting to believe that training in an Eastern fighting system would afford me superpowers. After Gracie had tapped out Shamrock my view altered, and I could see that this martial art (Gracie Jiu-Jitsu) was practical and actually did what it said on the tin.

Even if Shamrock had dealt a 'leaves on the track' defeat to Gracie's runaway train that night, the way we viewed martial arts would have changed regardless. It was obvious from the clumsiest of displays, that no martial art when used in a real fight had the beauty that was presented on the silver screen or in the dojo for that matter. And although Bruce Lee had lauded the benefits of simplicity, 'adapt or be destroyed', this new concept in pitting martial art against martial Art had highlighted the lies that had been apparent for thousands of years, the 'classical mess' that Bruce Lee had rallied against.

Whatever it was, this 'Ultimate Fighting' malarkey, I wanted to be a part of it. One thing was certain, I could never go back to my blinkered ignorance. Suddenly the world, or at least my perception of the martial arts and fighting in general made more sense.

My dad had always scoffed at traditional martial art systems. He used the analogy 'Karate doesn't work in a phone box', to illustrate a need for adaptability, i.e., fighting in confined spaces, an understanding of the environment, etc. He said that an art that is too flowery, has too many steps and relies on compliancy is impractical. Now all of these years later, I had to agree. It wasn't just the opinion of my dad, there were other martial artists that had started to question the practicality of their art.

The British pioneer of the 'less is more' movement was a Karateka and night club doorman called Geoff Thompson. His ground-breaking training routine consisted of pressure testing his art against non-compliant opponents that could use whatever they wanted in their attack. Geoff called this training 'Animal Day'.

Much like the Gracie's, Geoff wanted empirical evidence as to what might work in as close to a real attack as possible. Nothing was out of bounds. If the fight went to the ground (which it almost always did) the combatants continued to fight. It wasn't pretty to watch, and that was the point, but it soon became apparent that the staged self-defence routines that you had spent years perfecting where about as much use as a chocolate fireguard when the proverbial hit the fan. Add to the unpredictable nature of a real attack, the verbal aggression that often times proceeds violence and you had your own version of 'Karate doesn't work in a phone box'.

It wasn't the actual art my dad, or Geoff Thompson were criticising, it was more the application. A good reverse punch was as good a defence strategy as a good right cross if drilled properly and tested in this *alive way*. This was Bruce Lee's theory on the 'classical mess'. When we get hoodwinked into believing that the *pretty techniques* are effective.

My own research, if you like, had proven all of the above. I had never won a fight by standing on one leg (think Karate Kid), or with a high side kick to someone's head. My usual response to any threat was 'hit first, hit hard and keep hitting until the threat is over', something my dad had taught me from a young age. I had varying success with this strategy but just as the Gracie family were saying, 90% of fights go to the ground, and I'd certainly had my time rolling around on the cold tarmac.

Ground fighting was the unknown domain, a place where anything could happen. A well-placed thumb could blind, a bite could disfigure, and a grab of the genitals could ruin your chances of parenthood. And although my traditional Jujitsu class claimed to have the answers, it rarely came good for me. In the end, toughing it out or being prepared to go that bit further than the bloke you were rolling around the floor with, got me through. Now from out of nowhere came the answer, Gracie Jiu-Jitsu. An art so practical even my dad had to admit, might work in a phone box.

Anyway, on with the story. It wasn't long until UFC 2 and 3 were available. I had come late to the party and had watched the UFC 1 on bootleg VHS around 1995 maybe. UFC 2 and 3 only cemented my belief that Gracie Jiu-Jitsu was unbeatable, as Royce, this time with more style and panache, beat all comers with his trademark, takedown to submission finish.

Royce Gracie and his family were something of an enigma. There wasn't the wealth of information available back in the day. My understanding of the 'first family' of mixed martial arts (as it was later christened) was gleaned from these tapes. I knew for example that the patriarch of the family, Hélio Gracie, was the founding father. And that Gracie Jiu-Jitsu hailed from the tough streets of Rio, Brazil, where, by all accounts, Hélio and his sons, nephews and students, had been testing the art against all comers for 70 years or so.

This was the stuff of Hollywood movies. Royce's dominance of these early UFC contests was a sure thing really. After all, the art of fighting was the family business, and they had set out their stall for all to see. Fighting to the Gracies was as natural as breathing. This band of 'crazy' Brazilian's appeared to be latter-day evangelists of bare knuckle, drag out, spit and sawdust, good old honest to God practical martial art supremacy.

And whilst some of that was true, it wasn't the complete story. The Gracie family were no thugs, hardmen or loco Latino gangsters. They were erudite, decent and wry businessmen that just happened to have a style of Jiu-Jitsu that was not only very practical, but also very marketable. UFC 1, 2 and 3 were merely infomercials for the family product. The Gracies were selling their Jiu-Jitsu to the world, one fight at a time. And I, and many like me were eager to buy into the Gracie dream, but this was to prove a hard commodity to buy.

UFC 1 and its predecessors had opened the door for the Gracies in the USA. But in cold, wet and grey old England the door was firmly closed and would remain so for several years. I couldn't understand why any self-respecting Gracie Jiu-Jitsu black belt wouldn't jump on a plane and head straight for England, with all its green and pleasantness. We might not have the tropical climate, the golden sands that melted into translucent aqua seas, the beautiful bikini wearing... Hang on, I was starting to get it. At least the West Coast of America had all of that and more. In the North of England, we had Blackpool beach with its less than blue sea, cold winters and few and far between hot summer days that saw the vast population turning lobster red and drinking their body weight in lager. Rarely did you see a bikini, other than on a drunken stag intent on making the best of his last days of 'freedom' on the 'Golden Mile'. It was hardly paradise.

But if I thought the teachings of this 'new' Jiu-Jitsu were to stay out of my reach until a Gracie touched down on UK soil, I was to be pleasantly surprised.

Chapter 5

The Tale of The Tape

'The train is rolling but very slowly'

1996 (ish)

Halleluiah. The Gracie family, in their infinite wisdom had decided to put their Jiu-Jitsu system onto a series of instructional tapes (my prayers had been answered). In addition, they released 'Gracie Jiu-Jitsu in action'. A video of all of the 'challenge' matches that they had participated in prior to UFC 1. The tapes weren't cheap, but I reasoned, learning the system in its entirety was worth any amount of money (damn, at this point I would have done a deal with the Devil at the crossroads). After all, this was the key to the kingdom, I would be a Gracie Jiu-Jitsu expert in no time.

I had already started looking for a Gracie Gi, but the martial arts magazines, like Combat or Martial Arts Illustrated that were in vogue in the UK at the time were sparse to non-existent in their coverage of Gracie Jiu-Jitsu, let alone carrying ads for Brazilian jiu-jitsu apparel. But it was through one of these fine publications that I saw the tapes advertised. It was a no brainer that I would spend, what was then, a shed load of my hard-earned money on the entire set, with bonus 'in action' tape thrown in.

The wait was almost unbearable. Every morning I watched Postman Pot (so called because he had a liking for 'herbal' cigarettes) walk past my door, or occasionally deliver a letter I didn't want. What I desperately wanted was the tapes to arrive. I pondered for hours as to what magic they held. It felt like I was keeping the world's biggest secret, having withheld my purchase from my traditional Jiu-Jitsu friends. I wanted it to be a surprise when I tapped them with ease using my newly acquired Gracie Jiu-Jitsu moves.

In a way I pitied my Jiu-Jitsu brothers, they had failed to see the light. Some had watched the UFC tape, but were unmoved by its earth-shattering importance. They blindly went back to their 'classical mess'. I stayed more out of a need to train in something, to keep my hand in as it were, but more so for the time we got to practice ground fighting in the Randori. Grabbing someone's wrist and having them perform a flip that an Olympic standard gymnast would be proud of didn't hold the same satisfaction anymore, it was a necessary evil, something to endure before the rolling at the end of the session. I was a Gracie disciple now. Hélio was God in a Gi. Japanese Jiu-Jitsu was so last season, Brazil was where it was at.

And then one magical morning, as the sun strained through a slight gap in the curtains and the birds heralded the start of a new day, there came a knock on the door. I couldn't get out of bed and into my pre-arranged outfit faster. I had planned this moment with military precision, well, more like an expectant mother preparing for her waters to break. A pair of tracksuit bottoms hung over a chair, a *'Frankie Says Relax'* t-shirt, close to hand. I was ready. The knock could only be Postman Pot. Either him, or the bailiffs, and they had a less subtle technique for gaining entry. This was definitely not the blokes in black coming to repossess my TV. I took the stairs 3 at a time, hoping that Postman Pot wouldn't have got back in his van and drive my package back to the depot. That would be torture, knowing that the tapes were here, but out of my reach.

I opened the door and there stood Postman Pot in glorious technicolour. The grey pallor of his skin, the ill-fitting uniform, the glazed eyes and in his beautiful yellow stained fingers he held a parcel, my parcel. *'Sign here man'*. We had never really spoken before, but in that moment, his slightly high-pitched voice sounded like heavenly harps being plucked by an angel. It was only when I passed the hall mirror that I noticed my *'Frankie Says Relax'* t-shirt was on inside-out. No matter, in my hands I held the Holy Grail. Frankie could say whatever he wanted.

The packaging was torn off faster than a pass the (pills) parcel game in a room full of amphetamine heads. And there they were, *'Gracie Jiu-Jitsu Basics to Intermediate'*, plus the 'in action' bonus tape.

I loaded the 'in action' tape first, there was plenty of time to watch and learn the techniques later. The quality although poor was adequate, and the content proved again that this incredible system was unbeatable. I watched in wonder as one after another, Gracie family members took on a variety of ill-advised challengers. Each fight ended the same way, the Taekwondo or Kung Fu representative was taken to the mat, slapped around the chops before they rolled over into a choke hold, thus ending their moment of glory.

I loved the ease with which the GJJ guys beat their opponents, arm outstretched, lead leg stamping towards the knee before they closed the distance, body locked before a trip to take the stand-up fighter into deep waters. I laughed out loud (long before knowing what LOL was) as several, after tasting a quick and humiliating defeat, asked to go again. As if the outcome would be any different. They postured and confidently took up the pose of their respective art, desperately trying to conjure up the spirit of ninja warriors and the fearless masters that they had long revered.

Obviously, it didn't work out for them, and they were destined to be immortalised on these Gracie Jiu-Jitsu infomercials as those that had valiantly tried, but failed spectacularly, to dethrone the now first family of Brazilian jiu-jitsu.

Onto the techniques. I figured if I binge-watched the entire series, it would take about 7 hours, taking into account the occasional comfort break. The techniques were demonstrated by Rorian and Royce Gracie. Royce still looked moody, and Rorian, who until this point I was unaware of, had an assured confidence and explained the finer details with aplomb.

Their GJJ Gi's were the first thing that caught my attention. The Gracie Logo, tastefully displayed on each arm and on the back, was a simple triangle with stick like men performing a technique at its centre. It was the coolest thing I had ever seen. I wanted this Gi. In my naivety I was convinced that it was an essential acquisition in my quest to become a Jiu-Jitsu badass. It was a few hours in that I realised, with a somewhat sinking feeling, that the moves presented were similar to those I had learned in Japanese Jiu-Jitsu. I, of course was missing the whole concept that Rorian kept talking about, *'leverage'*.

The Gracie brothers kept talking about this concept, and I kept missing it. All I could focus on was the fact that there were no magical techniques, or at least not 7 hours' worth of stuff that would revolutionise my game, elevate me to the level of a 'Gracie'. I liked the clinch stuff at the start of the tapes, it seemed more practical than the block the arm stuff we did at my school. That could be implemented straight away. There was also a smoothness about Rorian's technique, he looked so relaxed.

Whereas the moves looked similar, it soon became apparent that they were performed differently. I could do a key lock for example, but compared to Gracie, my attempt looked like it needed oiling. It was stiff and unsophisticated in contrast to the beautifully executed example shown on the video. The Gracies were artists, their expression of a technique was a thing of joy to behold.

The first day after imbibing the entire catalogue of techniques, I was eager to get to the gym and try out the moves. I was teaching out of a sports centre in Cumbria and was lucky to have a few good training partners that seemed to enjoy the ground techniques that were apparent within the Bushi Kempo Ju Jitsu system that I held a black belt in.

We rolled, or as it was colloquially known, practiced Randori, after the technique portion of the class. But in traditional Jujitsu, the balance was very much biased towards the many self-defence techniques that made up the main curriculum.

I started to emphasise rolling more in my classes. Although with the gift of hindsight, we were very clumsy, and strength obsessed. There was very little in way of subtlety in the applications.

There was however a lot of head squeezing and forcing positions. If I were to try and compare what we were doing to the Gracie way, then it would be like Les Dawson's piano sketch, were he hits bum note after bum note before declaring that he is playing the right notes, just not necessarily in the right order.

In contrast the Gracie style was as precise as a Mozart symphony, not only were the notes in the right place, but they were fresh, new and revolutionary. I was really focused on getting the techniques off that I was seeing on the tapes. I drilled each move thousands of times. My training partners were in effect my guinea pigs and the dojo became my laboratory.

What I didn't realise was that the tapes were not able to convey the nuances that make the Gracie style so effective. I tried to start teaching the moves in class, becoming frustrated with the many knife and gun defences that my traditional system focused on.

I considered myself a Gracie disciple, the only thing I was missing was a messiah to show me the truth, the way and the light. But as the saying goes, be careful what you wish for.

Chapter 6

Rolls, Royce, and the Ultimate Gracie Machine

'The view from the carriage is amazing'

I wanted to immerse myself as much as I could in this almost mythical first family of Brazilian jiu-jitsu. The Gracie clan had seemingly taken the reputation of the traditional martial arts systems by the short and curlies and slam dunked it into a sea of self-doubt. Information was slow to hit this green and pleasant land. The only members of the family (at this point) that I had a sketchy knowledge of were Royce, Rorian and the elder statesman of the family, Hélio, and that information had come from the (now) 3 Ultimate Fighting Challenge videos that I had seen. I wanted to know the DNA and make-up of the rest of the train that had led Royce to the Octagon and into the UFC history books.

I first heard the name Rickson and learned of his place as 'the family champion' around the time that I watched UFC 2. He looked like he was built from a different mould to the other Gracies. He wore his hair in a ponytail for a start, but his physique was muscular, not like Arnold, more like Bruce. Rickson exuded an assured coolness that comes from a man at ease in his own space. An electric, almost zen like presence enveloped him like the *Ready Brek glow* that framed every schoolboy and girl in 1970's Great Britain.

I had seen Rickson fight; he was featured in the *'Gracie in Action'* bonus tape that I had watched a thousand times. He made short work of a behemoth called "Zulu" in a no holds barred fight in his native Brazil. The footage was grainy and didn't give much clue as to Rickson's Jiu-Jitsu mastery, but I just knew that he was the one; the chosen one. Royce may have been the fresh prince of the UFC, but I knew that Rickson was the undisputed king.

As more information filtered (albeit it slowly) through, I learned that Rickson was revered as a God amongst his peers. Legendary stories about his unblemished record, that was somewhere south of 400 plus wins, only gave credence to the myth. Even his siblings talked in hushed toned reverence about the man.

But wait, something was about to throw a spanner into the works, suddenly a new contender to the throne appeared. He also, like the rest of the clan, had a name that started with a R but pronounced as an H. Rolls (Holls) Gracie, he was the son of Carlos Gracie Snr, older brother of Hélio, and to many, the actual founder of Gracie Jiu-Jitsu. Confused?

Anyway, it turns out that Carlos, gifted his son Rolls to Hélio to bring up as his own. Rolls took to the family trade like a duck to water. He was, by all accounts, head and shoulders above anyone in the family in terms of his technical ability. What set Rolls apart from his cousins and siblings was his unquenchable thirst to improve on his base art. Rolls introduced Wrestling, Sambo and Judo to his training, he was fanatical in his quest to test his art against anyone and everyone.

Much like his father and uncle, Rolls set about proving himself and his art. But unlike those that went before, Rolls dared to enter into competition in the other disciplines he had added to his base art. He was wrestling wrestlers and trading leglocks with Sambo practitioners whenever an opportunity arose, and not only entering but winning.

And just when I thought I would have to relegate Rickson down to Prince in waiting, I learned that Rolls had died a few years earlier. Rolls was, by all accounts, a bit of an adrenaline junkie and had met his untimely demise in a hang-gliding accident.

Rolls had played a major part in the development of the younger Rickson who, like his late cousin, had incorporated other training methods into his daily routines such as yoga for its benefits to his suppleness and breathing exercises that he would later showcase in a documentary called 'Choke'.

I wanted to see Rickson take to the Octagon in place of Royce. By UFC 4 the traditional arts had all but disappeared from the roster. There was a new athlete to contend with, the 'Mixed Martial Artist'.

Chapter 7

The Emperor's New Clothes

'First stop, Lycra Street station'

The Gracies had unwittingly dealt a death blow to traditional martial arts, and in so doing, breathed life into a new form of combat, mixed martial arts (MMA).

As the UFC evolved, it became evident that this new breed of fighter had done their homework. The strikers had learned some jiu-jitsu and wrestling, and in turn the wrestlers had a rudimentary knowledge of boxing and kickboxing.

For Gracie Jiu-Jitsu, the UFC was a dream come true. The world was their oyster and they had done what they had set out to achieve; offering a pearl of wisdom that ground fighting was the martial art equivalent of the missing link.

Other organisations came to the fore. In Japan there was 'Pride', a mixed martial art show that preferred the more traditional ring as its amphitheatre and gave a platform to future MMA superstars such as Sakuraba et al.

In good old Blighty, it wasn't long before some domestic fight promoters jumped on the rapidly-gaining-momentum bandwagon. Soon even the diehard traditionalists started to take notice. Traditional Jujitsu schools, like the one I trained out of, started to market themselves differently. They used advertising jargon such as 'Gracie Style Jujitsu', bamboozling would-be BJJ wannabe students with cleverly worded mission statements that convinced them to part with their hard-earned cash, whilst giving the impression that they were training in the same system as their newfound hero Royce Gracie.

I researched anything and everything to do with Brazil. Up to this point, I had no clue about Brazil or for that matter any South American country, other than what I had heard in the mainstream press, that being, that Brazil was a pretty lawless place. It reinforced my thoughts that the Gracie Family must be the real deal, coming from a place with a reputation like that.

I scanned the magazines every month for any article or even a passing mention of the Gracies. But disappointingly, the two or three martial arts periodicals that I subscribed to where, in my opinion, biased towards the traditional systems. It was as if UFC 1 had never happened. Instead, the covers were graced by overweight, middle aged "masters' who looked like they couldn't fight sleep, let alone apply the street deadly moves they showcased in the technique section.

This new phenomenon Gracie Jiu-Jitsu, and now MMA, was to all intents and purposes, a whole new lifestyle choice, complete with must have fashion accessories. Gone were the days of uniform compliancy, i.e., everyone wearing the same white Gi, and woe betide any signs of individuality in the dojo. MMA was the equivalent of that cool kid at school, the one that defied the norm, dared to be different, even if it meant suffering the scorn of his/her peers. It stuck the middle finger up at authority, it was the punk rock of its generation, the rebel without a cause.

Sometimes, I would see an advert in the back of a magazine for training apparel. I was ecstatic when I found a pair of *Bad Boy Vale Tudo* shorts, and some Harbinger MMA gloves for sale. I had seen some of my growing legion of MMA heroes wearing the Bad Boy shorts. They were black budgie smugglers with a set of white fangs embossed on the butt cheeks. Coupled with a newly acquired Gracie Barra t-shirt with a motif of a Tasmanian Devil wagging a finger as if to say, *'don't fuck with me'*, I thought I looked the dogs' bollocks as I walked proudly into the training hall, adorned head to toe in my new purchases.

I more likely looked as camp as a row of tents and all that was missing from the scene was the Village People singing YMCA as the training hall doors were flung open and I sauntered confidently onto the mats.

My martial arts dress sense was certainly drawing some disapproving looks from my fellow Jujitsu practitioners. In my head I was way ahead of my time, a kind of free loving, paisley print, bandana type Jimi Hendrix guitar God amongst a sea of stuffy tuxedo wearing orchestra musicians. I felt sorry for my teammates. They had no clue as to the truth, the light and the way that I was now following.

I compared Rickson Gracie to a martial arts version of Jesus, he was crucifying himself for the sins of the traditional elitists that refused to believe in God (Hélio). I worshipped at the Gracie alter and the triangular logo was my cross. And Lycra it seemed, was the future.

Chapter 8

The Changing of the (old) Guard

'Changing at close legs and pray'

Choosing to ignore the stifled sniggers of my training partners (troglodytes), I focused on the handful of techniques I had picked up from the Gracie tapes that I had almost worn out through overuse. Japanese Jujitsu just couldn't hold my attention anymore. *'Get into my guard'* and *'let's roll'* became my new and favourite mantras. Gone were the days of back-to-back Randori sessions whereby whoever turned first would use strength and their considerable squeezing power to solicit the tap out, usually via a head lock.

I had always struggled to understand the 'back-to-back' logic whereby you started kneeling, it's not as if it had any real benefit. By starting face to face I would wrap my legs around my opponent in what the Gracies called 'the closed guard' and squeeze like a starving python holding onto its prey. It was a victory in my mind if no one passed my guard by the end of the 'roll'. It didn't really register that the person in the guard didn't have the techniques or skill set required to open, let alone pass the guard. Ego was my main opponent; I just didn't see it at the time. I was able to beat most, if not all, of my students anyway with or without Gracie jiu-jitsu. The proverbial big fish in a small pond.

What I really wanted to do was 'test' my new-found techniques against non-compliant opponents. I would hand pick the students that I thought might be a bit of a nightmare in a fist fight and have them wear the Harbinger 4-ounce MMA gloves. Their mission, if they chose to take it, was simple, 'try and punch me in the head'. Most chose to take the mission, and most seemed to enjoy the mission. I mean what's not to love, punching a bloke wearing eye wateringly tight black Lycra shorts with a pair of fangs on the arse cheeks.

The 'bout' would start in the same way, left arm extended, right fist covering my jaw. My lead leg would stamp towards the 'punchers' knee before I shot forward closing the distance and clinching tightly, head clasped to my opponent's chest.

Invariably, in the early days of perfecting my technique, I would eat a barrage of leather clad knuckle sandwiches. It was not uncommon to return home sporting a black eye, bloody nose or sore jaw, and sometimes all three. No matter, I was ready to take a few knocks in order to get my 'clinch and close the distance' badge in Gracie jiu-jitsu.

I quickly figured out that timing was everything. If I went too soon, I got punched in the head. If I went too late, I got punched in the head. I got into the habit of circling away from my would-be attackers' 'heavy' hand before the stomp and shoot were executed with the accuracy of a scud missile.

As the weeks went on, I was getting lit up less and less. I felt like Royce at UFC 1. The area I really struggled in was the takedown. So, after all the trouble to get the clinch, I was often swung around like a child in his fathers' arms. The classical Jujitsu throws didn't seem to work and Rorian Gracie made the takedown look so easy that I was sure I was missing something. Often times, even when I got the trip and ended up on top, my opponents' knee would have buried itself so far into my balls that it was in danger of becoming a permanent fixture.

Back to the drawing board. I re-watched the takedown video until I figured I had the missing link. I was getting the clinch but negating to bend my opponent backwards and step over as he fell. Once I sussed that, I was good to go.

The next phase was to introduce kicking into the mix. This proved a tad harder to master than I figured. As once you got the clinch, a crafty knee would cut up the centre line and again bury itself so far into your scrotum that it was eligible to claim tenancy rights. I was leaving the gym most nights talking in a falsetto voice, limping and looking like I had just gone ten rounds with Mike Tyson. All that and the Lycra too, what must the neighbours have thought as I struggled up the garden path?

But nothing worth having is ever meant to be easy. There was no way I was giving up. As Gloria Gaynor said, *'I will survive'*. I was after all a 'Gracie' disciple, I had the t-shirt to prove it.

Chapter 9

The Lion, the switch and the wardrobe (malfunction)

'Next stop, Worcester'

1998

It seemed that my attempts to change the way I trained wasn't exactly endearing me to my fellow traditional Jujitsu black belts. No one likes a smart arse after all. They, or at least some of them had seen the UFC tape and witnessed Royce Gracie's dominance over traditional martial arts. What they couldn't, or rather wouldn't accept, was that the style that Gracie had showcased was in any way superior to their beloved Japanese Jujitsu. They scoffed at the significance of the contest, deriding its merit as meaningless. They felt that it was a farce, a fix and that it was about as relevant as those pantomime wrestling bouts that featured on World of Sport every Saturday afternoon. Their system of Jujutsu was (in their opinion) not made, nor indeed 'safe', in a sporting context. But they saw similarities in the Gracie system and their own, stating that there was nothing new about it. Strange that they knew this without really seeing the art in its entirety. And strange too how quickly they used the Gracie's win and the UFC to promote their business model.

I didn't care. I wasn't going to be a sheep, blindly following and never daring to step out of line, to change direction. I had further alienated myself when I bought my first BJJ Gi. And although it wasn't a heavily badged typical Brazilian Kimono, it was a slap in the face to the hierarchy and a statement that I was moving away from the 'classical mess'.

I not only moved away from the Japanese system that I had practiced for the past 8 years, but I also decided that the only way I could progress in jiu-jitsu was to move. This wasn't an easy decision. It would mean leaving behind family and friends, not to mention a job and a thriving martial arts class.

The move, a couple of hundred miles, wouldn't magically place me amongst world class BJJ black belts, there simply weren't any in the country (yet). It would, however, place me closer to big cities, where any aspiring entrepreneurial BJJ black belt might decide to plant their flag.

If I needed another reason or a sign to change my martial art direction, it was given to me in glorious technicolour when Carley Gracie, 'The Lion' came over to the UK to teach a seminar. It wasn't cheap and the venue was quite a journey from my hometown, but hell and high water wouldn't keep me from attending. Combat Magazine had done a cover story on Carley, who until this point I had never heard of. He was, according to the article, undefeated and the 'true' champion of the family. I booked a place on the seminar and on the day made my way to the venue.

Upon arriving I was surprised to see a room full of martial arts black belts, Thai boxers, Jeet Kune Do practitioners and other assorted open-minded people wanting to see what 'Gracie Jiu-Jitsu' actually looked like.

We didn't have long to wait as the great man, resplendent in white Gi, black belt and white socks, walked onto the mats *(wait a minute, white socks)*. He was/is a big man, over 6 feet tall and of stocky, powerful build. He had a square, strong jaw and impeccable hair that had a touch of the 50's *rock and roll* era about it. His English was very good, having lived in the USA for many years, and he taught in an easy and friendly manner.

The day passed in a heartbeat, and like many seminars, I struggled to remember a lot of the content taught that day. But I did take away one technique that absolutely blew my mind, made me question how I had never thought of it and had me thirsting for more. The move was called 'the scissor sweep'. A staple of any self-respecting BJJ practitioner these days, but back then, it was as if I had witnessed the Wright brothers taking flight, saw Jimi Hendrix play for the first time or took the first step on the moon's surface hand in hand with Neil Armstrong singing *'Fly me to the Moon'*. Dramatic I know, but, that simple sweep, so easy yet effective, changed everything.

There was much about that day that I could talk about, but it is difficult to convey how much it meant to me to be in the presence of an actual Gracie, to learn directly from the source. It was 1998. I had been blustering about in the dark for a couple of years and all of a sudden there was a chink of light. Things were starting to happen. The rolling stone was at least rolling in the right direction.

I took a lot from that seminar, and even convinced myself that it was an important part of my BJJ development to wear white socks with your Gi. After all, what's good for the goose, or in this case the Lion, was good enough for me. It only dawned on me many years later and after training with other notable Brazilian jiu-jitsu illumine that the reason, he wore the socks was more to do with the typical inclement English weather.

Carley Gracie crossing the pond was a huge deal in terms of BJJ in the United Kingdom, I surmised that more BJJ royalty would follow. I knew that I had to find a way to make my move. But money was tight and at this point moving was still an impossible dream.

Chapter 10

If we build it, they will come!

'Me in the North, the action in the South. Damn, I got the wrong connection'

1998

Call me Nostradamus, my prediction that after Carley Gracie crossed the pond others would follow was so on the money, I considered setting up a stall on Blackpool Sea front and calling myself Gypsy Rose Savage. To my recollection, the first BJJ black belt to settle in England was Chen Moraes. Of course, he didn't venture *'oop North'* on arrival, but settled in our beautiful capital city, London.

I can't remember exactly when I first heard that Chen was on UK soil, or how for that matter, but there was an advert later on in one of the magazines advertising membership to the UK BJJ association (at least that's what I think it was called). After signing up, you received a cool triangular badge that you (your mum) could sew onto your Gi. Mine was worn with pride on my right sleeve. Chen's academy was called 'Anaconda BJJ' and the logo, surprisingly was a rather vicious looking (erm) Anaconda.

I wanted to up sticks and move to London then and there, but without money, a place to live and other kick in the teeth reasons, it just wasn't possible. London was as good as on the other side of the planet back in the day for me. I was frustrated but contacted Chen to ask if he had any plans for opening a satellite school in the back of beyond that was the North. His answer, unsurprisingly was no, but he told me that he planned on holding a UK and European BJJ competition and that I should sign up. That was a no brainer, when and where being the first words out of my mouth.

Chen had set up shop at the famous Budokwai Judo club in London and at the time of the first UK BJJ championships and had been teaching for around a year. London was ahead of the game, and I knew that the guys that were training under Chen would be the ones to beat.

My Jujitsu academy was flourishing but there was a spilt between students that wanted the traditional Japanese stuff and my little band of brothers that prayed at the altar of Hélio.

It was planned that 3 of my team would sign up and travel to the venue in Kensington. We ramped up our training regime. Personally, I was lifting weights, running 5 miles a day, rolling and drilling every day and when able to, I trained Judo at a local club.

I was no stranger to competition; I was a North of England Jujitsu Kumite champion and competed as often as I could. This competition felt very much a North vs South deal and we (Northern Monkey's) were at a disadvantage due to us not having a black belt coach at our disposal.

The date of the comp eventually came around and we set off to the big smoke on a coach that was filled with supporters. Listening to the chatter on the bus, I think people thought they were about to see something akin to the UFC. In truth, I don't think any of us knew what to expect that day, it was a brave new world. I was nervous, but excited to finally compete in Brazilian jiu-jitsu and although I knew that what I was practicing was a shadow of the real thing, I was quietly confident in my preparation.

We arrived at Kensington sports centre with plenty of time to spare. It was a beautiful day. The opulence of the area hit my Northern senses like a slap in the face with a Fleetwood Cod. This was a different world. I didn't see one flat cap wearing whippet, let alone a ferret or a racing pigeon. Mind I also didn't see any Lambeth walking Pearly King or Queens. I felt somewhat cheated.

Anyway, enough with the North-South stereotyping. On with the show. The competition hall was buzzing with excitement. I made a beeline for Chen and introduced myself. I was happy that he seemed to remember me from our conversation and was a really nice bloke into the bargain.

We quickly got changed and started stretching out, it felt like the scene from *Enter the Dragon* prior to the first bout. There was a hive of activity around the table that was being used to sort out the brackets. I decided to have a look at my category to get a feel of how many bouts I might have.

For the second time that day it was as if I was slapped in the face with a wet fish. There, next to my moniker was the name of my first opponent. It would have been fine had I not immediately recognised the person, and not only recognised the name, but greatly admired this person as one of the country's top martial artists. It was none other than the legend that is Rick Young. Rick was something of a national martial arts hero in the UK, regularly appearing on the covers of the martial arts magazines that I bought religiously each month. And not only was he an all-round superstar, but he had also travelled to America extensively to train under Rickson Gracie. If ever the bottom could fall out of my Gi pant world then this was it.

First round, first fight. What had I done to so anger the grappling Gods that they had forsaken me so? And to make matters worse, there was a bus full of 'fans' waiting to see their hometown hero crowned King in the big smoke, striking a blow for Northerners everywhere.

The fact that Rick was Scottish wouldn't matter to the eager students, their coach was about to face humiliation on the big show. And in front of Chen too. It didn't matter to them that Rick was a legend, or that he had graced the cover of so many martial arts magazines that I half expected him to have a row of staples running up his belly. No this was not good. I suspected (cynical I know) that Rick had been put opposite me to lessen the chances of a North vs North final. It mattered not as I stepped onto the mat as the baying crowd chanted 'Rick, Rick, Rick'. My supporters were drowned out completely as the great man took to the mats. I did what any man would have done, I played to the crowd, making the sign of the cross, like a condemned man accepting his fate. And then something clicked in me, this could be my David, toppling Goliath moment, I was damned if I was giving up before I had even started.

The crowd were at fever pitch as we gripped up, I had the advantage of prior knowledge and knew that Rick was a Judo black belt. I didn't want to be launched through the air, so I tentatively pulled guard, one foot went to Rick's hip, and I attempted, somewhat lamely, an armbar on hitting the tatami. Rick was onto my crafty little scheme and immediately tried to pass. I locked my legs around his waist in full guard and reaching inside his collar tried a cross choke. Again, Rick was one step ahead of me and thwarted my offensive move. People liken BJJ to a game of chess, in this bout I was definitely being out manoeuvred and in danger of finding myself in checkmate.

Rick passed to side control and attacked with a kimura. I saw it coming and placed my hands defensively by grabbing my belt. This, it seemed, was Rick's way of making me move my King into a precarious position. He took my Gi (my Gi, the cheek) and wrapped it around my wrist, locking my hand to my belt. What was he planning I mused, keeping a tight grip on the belt? I spun trying to re-establish guard, but that is the moment Rick was able to lever my hand free and apply the kimura. It looked very much like checkmate, and worse that my competition on that day at least was over, even if my humiliation just beginning. But whether it was pride or stupidity, I refused to tap as my arm was levered at an angle that would have seen it snap like a fallen autumn twig had the referee not intervened.

After bowing and the customary handshake I shuffled off the mat, trying not to meet the disappointed collective gaze of my students. I knew they would be mortified, but it was nothing compared to the feeling of utter despair that was coursing through my body.

Rick went on to win gold that day, and after the comp he approached to offer words of encouragement. He is a true gentleman and although he bettered me, I can honestly say it was an honour to compete against him. The loss, although hard to accept, turned out to be in the vein of one of those valuable life lessons we see in old episodes of The Walton's or Little House on the Prairie, *a rite of passage.*

We all took losses that day, but it was a great experience and watching the guys that trained under a legit BJJ coach only fuelled my ambition to do the same.

Chen is a huge part of the UK BJJ scene, he was instrumental in opening the flood gates, showing that it was possible to grow the art on British soil. I never got a chance to train under Chen, and that is a big regret, but he had a massive effect and influence on me. He gave me hope when there was none.

Not long after the first UK BJJ comp, Chen organised the European Championships. Again, in our great Capital City. This time I fared better taking a silver medal (Rick Young wasn't there). I was denied gold after facing a great grappler from Huddersfield called Andy Farrell. Andy was a machine.

Anyway, long story short, he finished our bout and my hopes of gold with the most brutal knee on belly I have ever felt. I must have looked in considerable pain, or maybe it was the same ref as my Rick Young bout, because for the second time in my short Jiu-Jitsu career, he stopped the fight and put me out of my misery. But at least I had tasted some success on the competitive stage and boy did it feel good. I was hailed as something of a conquering hero on my return to the frozen North, the local press even did a piece on my achievement. My student Maurice had also done well and took the bronze medal, so it was a double celebration for our back-water team.

Following the news that Chen was in the UK and we at last had a BJJ black belt in the country, things started to happen. The rolling stone was gathering momentum and a man that usurps Chen (in my opinion) as the founding Father of UK BJJ arrived on English soil, Mauricio Motta Gomes. The Gracie Barra black belt, and something of a legend, began teaching out of a disused custard factory in Digbeth, Birmingham. Mauricio is not just your average BJJ black belt, if such an animal exists. He received his *'Faixa Preta'* (black belt) from the late, great Rolls Gracie, who in his short life only awarded 10 people the much-coveted grade. To put this into some kind of perspective, getting a black Belt from Rolls is as rare as finding a hen with a full-on Simon Cowell grill of pearly whites.

Mauricio started to build a strong team of UK based students and soon there were a few home-grown blue belts.

You could tell the competitors that had access to a BJJ black belt, especially the newly opened Gracie Barra Birmingham students, they moved differently to everyone else and dominated their opponents with ease and skill. London and Birmingham were the UK epicentre's for BJJ back in the day and I desperately wanted to train under one of these coaches.

It felt like a small shaft of light was beginning to break through a previously black tunnel. Although not illuminating enough to show us the Jiu-Jitsu nirvana we craved, it was nether the less an exciting time in the history of UK BJJ.

There was a long way to go but at least our Founding Fathers had set the wagons in motion and two that I knew of (Chen and Mauricio) had planted their flags in this brave new world.

Mauricio's arrival piqued interest and the martial arts press started to take some notice. It felt like we were on the cusp of something big in the UK, and something big came in glorious technicolour in the shape of Renzo Gracie.

*It is worth noting that there were other BJJ high grades that were around at this time, and they were also important figures in the development of UK BJJ, I just don't know enough about them to include them in this part of the narrative.

Chapter 11

The Lone Shark!

'Life on the crazy train'

1999

If Carley is a Lion, then Renzo Gracie exemplifies the great white shark. He once said, 'The Lion might be the king of the Jungle but throw him in the Ocean and he becomes just another meal'. Renzo, aside from Rickson, is my all-time favourite member of MMA's first family. He is witty, articulate and as hard as a bag of nails. All that and a fearless warrior who steps up time and again to defend the Gracie legacy.

Renzo Gracie was brought over to give a seminar at the behest of Mauricio Motta Gomes. Mauricio was teaching in Birmingham so it made sense that the seminar would be in the Midlands again. The Gracies must have thought that all English people speak in a Brummie accent. Anyway, if I was excited about training with the Lion of the family, then Renzo was the icing on the Jiu-jitsu cake.

I travelled to Birmingham with my mate John, another Japanese Jujitsu black belt, and he wasn't really into Gracie Jiu-Jitsu but wanted a few ideas to add to his ground game. We made our way down the long and winding M6 and eventually found the venue (this was way before Sat Navs).

The seminar was held in a school of some kind that was housed in a suburban area of Birmingham. The car park was full to capacity, there were perhaps 100 people in attendance and a cursory glance around the training hall, evidenced at least 5 future MMA and BJJ standouts, including Ian Freeman.

In a corner, sitting on a windowsill, staring at the attendees was none other than the great Renzo Gracie himself. His face gave away little in the way of emotion and I remember him catching my eye and unnerving me with his intensity. John was less impressed and just laughed at my obvious 'hero worship' and little boy in a sweet shop demeanour. I was shaking with a mixture of nerves and excitement; I wanted the day to last forever. I wanted to remember every last detail, every nuance, every word uttered from this demigod.

We changed and found a place on the mats. John was a good Japanese Jujitsu black belt, but his understanding of BJJ was minimal. As a training partner he was good, due to the amount of time the classical systems teach compliancy. Everyone was busy warming up, stretching or just talking, I was watching. Renzo had still not moved, apart from picking up an apple which he proceeded to chew slowly and methodically.

I saw Chen and Mauricio at one side, at first talking and then as if answering my silent prayer, they started to roll. I couldn't believe my luck. The whole room stopped around me. In fact, the whole world in that moment ceased to exist, all eyes suddenly fixed on the BJJ black belts. I had never seen anything as beautiful in my life as this spectacle that was unfolding in front of my eyes. They moved effortlessly, and as if as one. Flowing with an energy I had never before witnessed. If you could see air, this is what it must look like.

It was obvious that Mauricio was the better of the two as he moved around Chen and dominated every position. Chen was skilled, there was no doubt about his ability, but he just didn't have the fluidity or grace that Mauricio was showcasing that day. If the seminar had been cancelled there and then I would still have felt that my money was well spent.

My mind was racing. I had, after what seemed like a lifetime of searching, been witness to 'real' BJJ. I was in two minds. One, I was elated at seeing these two great BJJ practitioners rolling, but also, I felt deflated. I knew in that moment that however hard I tried, I would never be 'that good', good enough to stop the world turning, good enough to inspire, good enough to be 'good enough'.

I don't believe I was alone in my feelings. Something magical had just happened, and for me it was as if I had borne witness to a miracle, not Jesus turning water to wine or walking on water, more giving the blind the gift of sight. It seems now, some 20 plus years later, just as awe inspiring. And although in a lot of respects I envy todays UK BJJ students for their ease of accessing a BJJ school, I wouldn't change that experience for the world. I can still see that roll, still feel the chill run through my spine, still feel the hairs stand on the nape of my neck, still feel that mix of excitement and fear, of hope and hopelessness.

Anyway, it was the most perfect start to a day as I can recall, Renzo jumped from the windowsill and walked towards the mat. The rolling stopped. We were called to order and after a brief introduction from Mauricio, Renzo Gracie spoke to us. He recounted with affection how Mauricio was his uncle and had helped him a lot on his BJJ journey. I listened to every word; it was as if the history of the Gracie family was being told for the first time. Renzo spoke with humility, humour and great insight, and we listened.

Renzo had a really approachable manner and taught with an ease that comes with complete mastery of a subject. I don't recall all of the techniques that Renzo demonstrated that day, apart from the arm bar from guard. This part of the day is etched in my memory so indelibly that it can never be erased and that is down to my friend John, who until this part in the narrative had only really come along for the ride.

We had been practicing the technique for a good 5 minutes when out of the blue, and without warning, John shouted across the packed, yet at this point eerily quiet, hall, *'Rickson, have you a minute?'* My face turned a shade of red that was somewhere between beetroot and the purple tinge of a heavy drinker's nose. I was in short, mortified. Not only had John got Renzo's name wrong, he might as well have gone the whole hog and brought a megaphone to announce his faux pas.

Talking out of the side of my mouth in that not-so-subtle way that the British do when trying desperately to be subtle, *'It's Renzo you prick'* I whispered. 'And for the record the 'R' is pronounced as a 'H', as in fucking Henzo and Hickson'. It felt like the whole room in that moment was listening to our little tête-à-tête, I could feel the burn of 100 pairs of eyes burrowing into my soul. I could almost hear their collective thought, 'what a pair of knobheads'.

John just smiled at me like an oaf, which further infuriated me, and then as if the most natural thing in the world, Renzo was standing next to us. *'Erm, Renzo, can you check I'm getting this armbar right?'*, said John, still pronouncing the bloody 'R'. It was, I knew, an act of defiance for my remonstration and calling him a 'prick'. Renzo, if offended, didn't give away his anger as he smiled broadly and said, *'Of course my friend.'*

John went through his demonstration which to my chagrin was as good as it gets. Renzo again smiled and said, *'That's better than me, my friend.'* What the actual fuck. Here I was, the Gracies number 1 fan, a man that knew his Rickson from his

Renzo, a devotee of the art, too awe inspired to speak in front of Renzo, let alone show him my arm bar. And here was John. Not arsed either way if he was in the company of Renzo Gracie or Gracie Fields, getting complimented on his technical skill. If there was a God, now would be the time to smite me with a bolt of lightning, either that or turn me into the jack ass I felt like.

My cheeks were still burning but I tried to downplay things by laughing a little too loudly and shaking my head as if to say, 'he's not with me, I just paired up with him because there was no one else', which might have worked, if not for John announcing, 'there you go Sav, he didn't mind being called Rickson'.

My newly paling cheeks started to heat up for a second time in as many minutes. It had, apart from 'Rickson gate', been an incredible day up to that point, but the best was yet to come. At the end of the seminar there was a question and answer, everyone loves a good Q&A.

After a rather awkward silence, someone found the minerals to ask a question, '*I get caught in side control a lot and find it hard to escape*', came a voice from the back. All heads turned as if one. The man asking the question wasn't particularly big or for that matter small. Renzo fixed him with a look before saying '*Ok, let's see*'.

He scanned the room before settling on the biggest guy in the room. A bemouth with a shaved head and cauliflowered ears (a rare sight back in the day, the ears not the shaved head).

'You my friend'. Renzo gestured for the unit to come over. '*Put me in your best side control, do you know this position?*' Know the position, this fella looked like he could hold water in his side control.

Renzo lay down and his cauliflowered assistant dutifully got into position. The size difference between Renzo and the unit was immense. You could hear a pin drop as Renzo wriggled about beneath this man mountain.

What seemed like a lifetime went by, only interrupted by the occasional giggle from Renzo, as the behemoth held on for dear life. This was starting to feel very uncomfortable. What if Renzo couldn't escape? I could feel a bead of sweat breaking through my forehead and slowly tracing down my face. My heart was beating so hard I was sure that the whole room could hear it.

Beside me, John, who had just whispered something *like 'I don't think Renzo is getting out of this.'* The fact that he was still mispronouncing the name suddenly seemed so trivial, after all this was a disaster of epic proportions.

And then it happened, just when I was at the point of covering my eyes and praying for the ground to open up, the unit appeared to take flight. Renzo spun out of the hold down and as if to make every wrong in the world right, he applied an arm bar to finish his demonstration. The whole room gave a collective *'ooh'*. The unit smiled and sheepishly made his way back through the crowd. I could have jumped to my feet and danced. *'There you go John, oh ye of little faith, Henzo (emphasising the correct pronunciation) was never in any danger. That's the problem with you 'trad' guys, you just don't understand how effective BJJ is.'*

The seminar was then brought to a close. What a day. John and I made our way back *'oop North'* in relative silence, each reflecting on the day's events. For me there was the roll between Chen and Mauricio and the sight of Renzo sending the unit into orbit. For John I'm sure it was Renzo's praise of his arm bar.

To have the opportunity to train under someone of Renzo's stature was a dream come true. To put it into perspective, it was akin to having a football lesson from Pele or David Beckham, but more Pele.

This was a seminal point in my development in BJJ. Not only was it evident that things were starting to happen, but there seemed a beginning of a community amongst the BJJ wannabes in the UK. It seemed like we were a part of a daring and stylish underground movement that only we 'got'. A bit like the Punk Rock years in the UK, before (that horrible word) commercialisation, took away the essence of everything that was good about the movement. And like any new thing, there was an excitement attached. It felt like we (the few) were part of a revolution. It was our job to make this movement work, we knew that once we did, then it would ultimately not be 'just ours', it would belong to the masses and open to commercialisation.

But we also knew that we didn't own this. We were only the caretakers, gardeners if you like, that had helped to plant a seed. A seed that would one day grow into a mighty oak tree. But back then we just didn't realise how the art would grow, or even if it could grow.

There is a part of me that is thankful for the stubborn streak that runs through me. I wouldn't, couldn't give up, it isn't in my nature. But we all like a bit of encouragement and the encouragement I was about to get was a tad more than 'a bit'.

Chapter 12

God speaks and I listen

'Finally, on the right track'

The Noughties Circa 2000-2001

The coverage of BJJ or MMA in martial arts magazines although still sparse, was getting better. I recall seeing an interview with Royler Gracie around this time and was astounded to see that his email address was included at the bottom of the page. After nervously pacing the living room floor for a minute or two, I decided to reach out and email him. I wasn't convinced the email wouldn't be answered by some admin, but I figured I had little to lose. My email went something like this:

'Hi Royler, just a quick line to say that I am a fan of your family and hope one day to train with you. I live in the UK and at present there is no BJJ available other than the tapes that Rorian and Royce have made available. It is very frustrating and at times it feels that we (the UK) will never be in a position to learn your family's art properly. Do you have any advice on how I can progress without a legitimate teacher?

Best regards

Gary'

I didn't expect a reply, I was venting my frustration really, but you could have knocked me down with a feather when this appeared in my inbox.

'Hi Gary,

Thanks for the kind words. My advice is don't give up. Jiu-Jitsu will come to the UK and in the meantime keep practicing the techniques. All the best.

Royler'

The email response is paraphrased as I have long since lost it, but the content and advice are as close as I can recall. It may seem trivial to some, but this email spurred me on, it gave me hope in what seemed like a hopeless situation.

I wondered then, as I do now, what it must be like being born into the Gracie family, to be a part of that dynasty. The pressure must be immense. I mean what if you were the one Gracie that just didn't get Jiu-jitsu at all. You hated it.

It draws parallels to the film Billy Elliot where the story's namesake wants to be a ballet dancer in a town full of tough miners. I could relate somewhat to the situation (not the ballet part). I dreamed of achieving something that seemed so far from my reach. Brazilian jiu-jitsu black belts were the toughest *Mo Fo's* on the planet. The actual belt took at least 15 years to get and that was training with a top coach. We had no one. I didn't even know any blue belts at this time, it felt like a very solitary pursuit. It wasn't as if there was a help line to call. Lenny Henry and Bob Geldof wouldn't be doing a fund raiser to deal with this crisis anytime soon.

I had heard that a guy from the UK had travelled to the Gracie Academy in America and was a blue belt. Another guy, Rick Young, one of the country's top martial artists was also making regular trips abroad to train with the Gracies. What was I doing wrong?

How I wished I had been born into a rich family (not that I think either of the aforementioned were). I could travel the world training BJJ all day and sipping martini's (shaken not stirred) in the evening, whilst surrounded by a bevy of beautiful women all vying for my attention. Oh well there is nothing wrong with dreaming.

My reality was somewhat north of the fantasy, I had about as much chance of travelling to America and training with the Gracies as I did of winning *spot the ball*, not that I played, which I think holds a lesson for us all. If we are to achieve what many will not, we have to do what others will not. You have to *be in it to win it*, so to speak.

I'm sure that Rick Young and Marc Walder made massive sacrifices to train abroad, but that is why they were the first UK BJJ black belts. They not only dared to dream, but they made their dreams a reality.

Anyway, I didn't have big enough balls to give up everything and travel to some far-flung destination. At this point I had only ever been on an aeroplane a couple of times and that was for cheap package holidays. I was barely able to put food on the table and pay the rent. But even though Brazil or America was a bridge too far, I could move away from the area I lived in and try at least to be in the right place at the right time when a BJJ black belt, or even a blue belt showed up in one of our bigger northern cities.

So, there I was heading down the M6 in search of enlightenment, all my worldly goods packed into my little Red Ford Fiesta. It was a cold winters day; I remember that because my car heater was on the blink and I was wrapped up like an Egyptian mummy, resplendent in a large overcoat, scarf, fingerless gloves and a kind of deer stalker hat.

I didn't really have a plan, but what the hell, I would be fine. When I say I didn't have a plan, that isn't absolutely true. I planned on training with a JKD instructor that had done some BJJ as part of his curriculum-based training under Dan Inosanto (Bruce Lee's original student). It wasn't ideal, but at least I would be training in a more focused environment than I was used to.

I was also planning on attending university (so I suppose I did have a plan). If I was going to travel and train BJJ for the rest of my life I would need a good income, at least until I made it as a fighter and BJJ coach.

I have always been a dreamer, and thank God I am. Had I listened to my parent's advice to 'stop daydreaming', I wouldn't have had the courage to let my heart rule my head, I would have taken the easy road, got a job that required zero creativity, lived in a house that was 'safe', married the girl next door and go lemming-like over the cliff with the rest of the *cradle-to-grave* and *nothing-inbetweeners* that lay broken on the rocks below, along with their hopes and dreams.

Anyway, I was and am for my sins, a daydream believer. I always felt there was something more than the drudgery of the nine to five. A life spent staring at a box, fantasising about the lives of others, whilst running on a never-ending hamster wheel. No, that wasn't for me. I knew that I had to move out of my comfort zone, swim in a larger pond, test myself. I wanted to feel alive, to be in a situation where I had to adapt or be destroyed, nothing comes from comfortable. In order to grow we have to get out of the shade, feel the sun on our face.

The sun on my face turned out to burn quite badly, as I quickly discovered that walking into an established gym, full of tough young lads all intent on 'making an example' of the newbie was akin to being thrown into a lion's den. A hungry lion's den.

I managed to hold my own during the rolling at the end of the session, however, when the coach called time and put me in the middle of what I now understand to be a *'Shark Tank'*, I knew I was being tested. Maybe this was a kind of initiation. One after the other, my rolling partners did their best to catch me in a sub and each failed. Little did they know that I had overdosed on the Gracie tapes and done this kind of rolling so much that it wasn't really fazing me. In fact, I was loving it.

After about 15 minutes of 'fun', the coach decided that I needed a 'real challenge'. And much like Bolo stepping up to dismantle the negligent prison Guards in Enter the Dragon, here he was, my 'challenge'. He was older than most on the mat but still considerably younger than me. He was built like a brick outhouse and at over 6 feet tall, towered above all. And here I was, panting like a dog, sweating like Lester Piggott waiting for his tax bill and totally knackered. What could go wrong?

The behemoth wasted no time and rushed towards me, obviously smelling blood. I pulled guard. If this gym champion was going to defeat me then I sure as hell wasn't going to take it lying down, even though technically that's exactly what I was doing.

I locked my legs tightly around my nemesis' waist and pulling forward, broke his posture, and hugged him tighter than a pair of Chuck Norris's stretch Wranglers. He was desperate to pass the guard, but I was equally desperate to hold, tire him out a bit and level up the playing field.

We stayed in this position for a good five minutes, neither giving up on their game plan. The Desperate Dan grade decided to up the ante and by digging his very pointy elbows into my thighs, managed to open my guard.

A quick glance at the head coach saw that a wry smile had slipped past his thinly veiled facade and his delight was shining as bright as a Blackpool illumination on a dark November night.

Backing up to gain the advantage of distance I quickly locked onto my opponents' neck with a guillotine choke, squeezing for all I was worth, I could hear the gurgle and gasps for air as my opponent desperately tried to prise his slowly turning purple head (ooh missus) from my death grip.

Eventually I had to release my hold, my arms had burned out and I was good for nothing. Behemoth passed to side control and after almost ripping my now limp right arm out of its socket, I had to admit defeat. Slapping hands, I struggled to my feet and after taking my place in the line-up, bowed and shook hands with the rest of the team.

It was only when I was in the changing room later, struggling to get dressed, that my enthusiasm was curbed somewhat when the instructor shouted into the dressing room to his 'champion', *'What did you catch the tosser with?'* He obviously had assumed, wrongly as it transpired, that I had left the building. His face was as red as mine, although for different reasons, as I emerged from the room and without a flicker of emotion said, *'thanks for the lesson'*.

I walked out and never returned. And not because I had been bettered, that didn't bother me, it's what I needed. It wasn't even the label of being a 'tosser' (if the cap fits and all). It was the fact that this coach, who had demonstrated the techniques so efficiently hadn't done his own dirty work and 'taught the tosser a lesson' himself. That and the two-faced response. I can forgive many things, but falseness and insincerity are not my bag. My search for grappling enlightenment continued. Back to the drawing board.

My next stop was a dilapidated old building in Manchester's Piccadilly district that housed a martial arts gym called *'Defence Unlimited'*. As rough as sandpaper and not a particularly welcoming place. Nonetheless, it had that authentic *'old school'* gym feel to it; a certain charm that has attracted fighters for decades.

You literally took your life into your hands just getting up the rickety old staircase, the building looked like it should have been condemned. It was certainly no state-of-the-art facility.

The grappling and MMA classes were taught on the top floor, the second floor was the home of Steve Powell's JKD training group. I had heard about the Defence Unlimited (DU) team through the articles that the head coach Karl Tanswell had written for Martial Arts Illustrated (MAI). Karl was very knowledgeable and his column in MAI was always my favourite part. The DU team had won quite a few tournaments and had a great reputation, as did Karl and his then right-hand man, Gavin Boardman. There was also a BJJ blue belt called Colin Robinson who taught a couple of nights a week out of the top room.

Karl and Gavin taught No Gi Submission Grappling, and this was what I started with upon enrolling in the classes. I suppose I was dipping my toe in the water before trying the actual Gi classes although, given my obsession with Gracie Jiu-Jitsu, I am baffled all these years later as to why. The No Gi sessions were by and large very busy and the Gi classes not so much, so that might be why I chose them.

I started training in the No Gi classes a couple of days a week and on a Saturday morning. These were tough sessions and at the end, if I had any energy left, I would stay for Colin's classes.

Colin was a really technical coach and although nowadays when black belt instruction is more readily available, back in the day a blue belt in BJJ was God.

I learned so much during my time at Defence Unlimited and even started doing a weekly private session under Karl. Manchester was a good hour's drive from my new digs, and money was tight, but I was determined to rustle up enough cash to pay for the training, even if it meant going without daily living essentials.

In-between the course work at university, I was working as a security guard on a large caravan park. The money was terrible and the hours long. I started around 9.00pm and finished at 7.00am. A gruelling regime that was starting to take its toll, but I needed to train. I knew that it would be worth it in the long run.

Some weeks I was heading to Manchester, taking a class, driving straight to my security job and working straight through until getting to uni to attend a lecture. I slept a couple of hours before repeating the whole process.

At Defence Unlimited there was a wealth of talent. Saturday mornings were always a battle ground with some epic drilling and rolling. I loved the rolling more than the drilling but knew that it was a necessary part of the training. There was a wrestler that showed up most Saturdays called Ian Bromley. He was the archetypal grappler. Both ears looked like they had been through a mangle, he was strong and fit and had crazy skills. I loved rolling with Ian as he always made me feel like a complete novice. Sometimes I might get a good position, only to find myself sailing through the air and unceremoniously dumped onto my back before some of the most painful submissions I have ever felt applied. Ian was a Catch Wrestler. I hadn't heard of this style until I met Ian and was introduced to its broad array of finishing (very painful) holds, but I was very impressed nonetheless.

Defence Unlimited had a very eclectic approach. I learned how to shoot, arm drag, apply a two-on-one and was introduced to other great wrestling concepts at this gym. Things I still use and teach today.

I decided that an easier way of making money was to teach again. I could work on the new techniques I had been taught at DU and bring Karl to the gym to give the occasional seminar. I decided that nearby Lancaster was the best place to teach out of. And instead of calling my style Jujitsu and recreating what I had done in the past, this new club would be more MMA focused.

*NB- Karl Tanswell, Colin Robinson and Ian Bromley are all deceased now, but each played a huge part in the development of BJJ in the UK and each helped me personally. RIP.

Chapter 13

A storm in a sports cup

Stop the train I want to get off

2002

Lancaster is a beautiful city. The historic castle that doubles as a prison stands strong and proud above picturesque tea rooms, *'olde worlde'* pubs and antique shops. But beneath the prim and proper surface, Lancaster was a city at odds with the idyllic image and surprisingly, at one time, had one of the highest murder rates in the UK (demographically). In short, it had, like most villages, towns and cities in the UK, a darker underbelly.

I found a room in a sports centre that was between Lancaster and the neighbouring town of Morecambe, the ideal place to hone my MMA and jiu-jitsu skills. Now all I needed was a student.

As the saying goes *'ask and you shall receive'*. One day, in walked Nigel: balding, be-speckled and looking more at home sorting out overdrafts and mortgages than punching and choking people out. Looks can be deceptive and it didn't take me long to impart some of the *'bread and butter'* techniques that I knew.

A lot of the early curriculum I taught to Nigel, and later the growing student intake, was based on the limited Gracie Jiu-Jitsu I knew, mixed with the stuff I was learning at Defence Unlimited. I had already trained quite extensively in Thai boxing and kept some of the more practical techniques from the Japanese Jujitsu system that I had a black belt in. We concentrated mainly in grappling without Gi's as it was more in keeping with the MMA vibe that we had going on. The name of the academy went through several changes until we settled on *'The Grapplers Academy'*.

Training was brutal. We sparred full contact and it wasn't surprising as a result that we had a high turnover of students. Most came once or twice before deciding that the black eyes and the occasional dislocations weren't for them.

The Grapplers Academy became a band of brothers. We trained hard and partied hard, often going on drinking sessions that lasted into the early hours and once or twice ended with a mass brawl.

There were some real characters that walked through our doors. Most wanted to challenge us, to see if this 'MMA' was any good. Usually these *have-a-go Henry's* were just untrained wannabe hard men. Most couldn't fight sleep, let alone mix it up with lads that put in the hours on the mat, sparring hard on a regular basis. In the early days I would step up to meet the challenges, but as the rest of the lads grew in skill and confidence, it didn't matter who applied the choke or arm lock that ended the tough guys hopes of boasting rights. We never brutalised any of these weekend warriors, a quick shoot takedown, a couple of gentle slaps and a choke usually did the trick.

It was all very much in keeping with the *Gracie in Action* tapes. Some, the newly humbled, actually signed up for lessons. Most left with dented pride and a newfound respect for MMA.

There were some really tough and talented lads that trained out of the Lancaster gym, James Lamb, Sergio Zappone and his brother Shay Walsh (who became a British MMA star), Gary Hill, Gavin, Nigel, German Ronnie and the toughest little fella I ever met, Andy Steele, whom the phrase *'it's not the size of the dog in the fight, but the size of the fight in the dog'*, could well have been written for. We might not have been a big team, but we all wanted to fight, to compete. It was a magical time for me, I had a group, albeit small, of like-minded lads that liked to mix it up.

After a while, we introduced the Gi to our training, but I still wasn't confident enough to teach BJJ. I was after all a white belt, that at this point had attended a Carly and Renzo Gracie Seminar and the odd class under Colin Robinson.

My *wake up and smell the coffee* moment happened one bright sunny day, a year or so after opening the Grapplers Academy when a new face walked into the training room. He certainly looked the part in rash guard and grappling shorts and a groin guard (at least I hope that was a groin guard). He told me that he had trained in America under Pedro Saur, a Rickson Gracie black belt and further he was a blue belt in BJJ. Excited was an understatement. I was a little apprehensive showing technique in front of a bona fide BJJ exponent but managed to get through the session and to the rolling/sparring section. I made a bee line for BJJ blue, now known to me as Darren. We rolled for a good 10 minutes, neither catching the other. I noticed how relaxed his game was. I was still using far too much strength, a throwback to my Japanese Jujitsu training. Darren was friendly and respectful after the roll and invited me to his class in Blackpool later that week. He had only just started teaching a Gi session out of Alan Scott's martial arts academy and his numbers were still quite low.

Blackpool Rock n Rolls

I turned up early for the lesson and Darren asked if I would roll with him again, only this time in the Gi. We gripped up and Darren pulled guard. I recall him wrapping my arm in what I now know to be the lasso guard, and me sailing through the air before being unceremoniously dumped onto my back and a swift choke applied. *Wow, I don't think that was a fluke*, I recall thinking as my ego deflated like a pinned balloon. Time and again I was swept, arm barred, choked and generally humiliated on that mat, but boy, oh boy did I love the experience. In No Gi I was confident, but in the Gi, against someone that knew what they were doing I was like Bambi on ice.

Darren was the first BJJ coach in Blackpool and his class attracted some really good people. Alan Scott who owned the gym and was a phenomenal martial artist in his own right offered me a coaching position at the gym as the MMA coach. It would mean handing over the Lancaster gym to James, Sergio and Andy, but they were all more than capable of running things. I in turn could then focus on setting up in Blackpool and importantly train under Darren Harrop in the Gi.

These were heady times and training in a martial arts academy that had everything under one roof presented some great sharing and learning opportunities. I was teaching a private session one afternoon and sharing the mat with two of the Wing Chun instructors. I could see that they were watching intently in-between practicing techniques.

At the end of the session, I asked one of the instructors to show me the straight blast chain punch from their system as I had always thought it very practical. After a brief instruction, the coach said that I would get a better feel for it if we sparred.

I didn't need asking twice but told the Wing Chun coach that I would only use grappling and he could do whatever he wanted from his art.

We squared off, him in an orthodox Wing Chun stance, me, arm outstretched, right fist protecting my jaw as in the *Gracie in Action* pose. Before I could utilise my lead stomp into clinch technique, the Kung Fu guy rushed forward, his fists of fury darting out at an alarmingly fast pace towards my face, I had no choice but to back pedal, my arms covering my grill and absorbing the impact of his knuckles.

One or two punches managed to sneak through, but there wasn't much power behind them. To say this bloke was in a short, and what looked to be an awkward stance, he could certainly move, and not just forwards. I attempted to thwart his attack by changing direction, but he stuck like glue and continued his barrage of punches. I was now seriously regretting telling him that I would not use any strikes. I couldn't believe he wasn't getting tired; this Kung Fu dude was like a Duracell bunny.

After blocking another couple of his punches with my face I decided that I needed to meet force with force, after all I had little or no clue as to any other way of stopping him. I changed level as two rapid punches whistled over my head and drove forward, meeting his body with full impact as I did so. My arms circled his legs, and my right foot trapped his lead foot. He toppled to the mat, his fists still pumping the air like a stoner at a Van Halen gig. I scrambled past his legs and took full mount. Welcome to my church. I reached around his neck and locked him in. His reaction was, as I expected, he bucked harder than a stallion at a rodeo. I hung on for dear life, I mean how much more energy could Hong Kong Phooey have left. Morals are all well and good but when you are out to prove a point, they are dropped faster than a bride's nightie. I transitioned into a high mount and slapped my now tiring opponent around the chops. I could see he was disappointed by my change of plan. He tried to turn, just like the cast of *Gracie in Action* had done and I, much like the Gracies had, sunk in a choke. Game over.

I think we both learned a valuable lesson that day, although I am at a loss to remember mine. Ah yes, that's it, when getting into a bare-knuckle exchange with a very competent Kung Fu exponent, don't agree not to punch or kick. If you are going to fight, know your opponent and their game plan. Anyhow, I developed a healthy regard for Wing Chun, and I still really like that straight blast technique that I learned all those years ago, even if it was the hard way.

My time teaching out of Alan's gym was the equivalent of doing a master's degree in martial arts. It was a melting pot of talent, I was surrounded by people that really knew their art. Alan had travelled and trained in China, he could generate a scary amount of force with a punch that was no more than an inch from its target. His stance was so strong that you just couldn't move it. I was like a kid in a candy store. This was a time of sharing techniques, challenging beliefs and generally growing as martial artists.

My 'sparring match' with the Wing Chun Guy had certainly opened my eyes as to the danger of being a one trick pony and worse, a pony that was wearing blinkers. There were more 'learning' opportunities to be had. I was, after all, a realist. I wanted to test myself and my art in an empirical way. Sitting on the side-lines and telling my students to do this or that technique, knowing full well that it was as much use as a chocolate fireguard in a live situation was not for me, not my style. I wanted my 'art' to be a true reflection of my experiences. As Bruce Lee said, 'boards don't hit back'.

What does hit back are like-minded people. Around this time, I put on the gloves with competent boxers, laced up my wrestling boots with gnarly eared old school *Catch-as-Catch can* wrestlers and took many a bruising leg kick from Thai boxers.

One thing I learned above all else from these 'research' sessions, was never to take an opponent at face value. The 9 stone boxer was capable of hitting you flush on the jaw with every ounce of his 9 stone. The gnarly eared old wrestler would prove that age is just a number and that a key lock, with some minor adjustments, was a whole different level of pain. My jiu-jitsu wasn't at the level that I could best represent it properly. I had a rudimentary understanding of what 'might' work in different ranges, but it was apparent that I had a long way to go before I could fully integrate all that I was being exposed to.

And of course, there was nothing like testing your skills against someone that was intent on causing you a world of pain. I used to bring people into my gym that had fearsome reputations, not just other martial artists, but doormen etc., I wanted to be put under absolute duress, to get used to discomfort. Like the saying goes *'what doesn't kill you, makes you stronger'*. These 'sparring' sessions were absolutely brutal. We didn't have the knowledge as to how to train scientifically. It was a case of gumshield in, gloves on, lets fight.

One session stands out and illustrates this naivety. I was doing some stand up sparring with a local doorman that had some training in martial arts. We were in a boxing ring that was so small you literally wouldn't be able to swing a cat in (not that I advocate feline cruelty). Anyway, after a few rounds my sparring partner decided that the gloves we had on were hindering things and suggested we 'lose the leather' (gloves not trousers in case you were wondering). Like I said earlier, this was way before sports science had revolutionised training methods, and long before those health and safety killjoys had us terrified of doing anything remotely risqué. So, we went at it. In the smallest space imaginable, standing toe to toe, punching lumps out of each other for 5 or 6 rounds. It's amazing how quickly you learn to keep your hands up and move your head when a 19 stone bloke is trying to punch a new hole in your face. We both took our lumps that day, and we both laughed about it afterwards and importantly it was another great lesson learned.

In grappling terms, I learned a lot from competing or just rolling with quality people. One roll that stands out was during one of the first open mats I had ever attended. Karl Tanswell had organised it as a way of bringing the fledgling grappling community together. If by 'bringing us together' his intention was all out war, then he achieved his aim. This was no 'we are all one', love and peace affair. It was a time when there was still a degree of suspicion and 'one-upmanship' amongst the relatively small numbers that made up the 'grappling/MMA community'.

If I remember correctly, the event was held at the Sugden Sports Centre in Manchester city centre. There was a healthy turnout and a broad array of the latest must have lycra on display. As a man in his early 30's, I felt old as I scanned the youthful 'competition'. The whole thing felt a bit awkward at first, groups of men and a few women stood in their 'comfort bubbles', nervously eying up (as was I) the rest of the room. In the centre of the hall, the mats had been laid out ready for the 'friendly' rolling to commence.

The unfolding scene reminded me of a school disco, where groups of shy teenage boys stood awkwardly on one side of the room and the girls giggled and waited patiently to be asked to dance on the other.

After a few words from Karl the event could get under way. It was a cautious start, most grabbed someone from their own gym to warm up. I paired up with some tattooed and heavily muscled lad that told me he had travelled up from Wigan or there about. We had a great roll, the lad was a handful, but I detected from his style that he had a limited vocabulary of submissions. Don't get me wrong, his control was really good as was his movement, but I didn't feel threatened by the few attempts he made to guillotine or crank my arm into a figure four lock. I used my much drilled and efficient triangle to solicit the tap. At the end of the roll, we shook hands and scanned the mat for someone new to test our skills on. My eyes fell on a man that must have been in his 50's. I hadn't noticed him up to this point but felt an immediate respect for him. In my mind I had concocted a story that he was one of those people that didn't really see age as a barrier to trying something new. Probably got sick of badminton and had heard about this 'new' thing, MMA and jiu-jitsu, and thought 'what the hell'. He had clocked me too and made a beeline in my direction. 'Great' I thought, I came here to have some good, hard rolls, not share the mat with a bloke that looked more at home in a Werther's Originals advert. Looks can be deceptive and it's a dangerous game to make assumptions.

The 'Werther's Original' man turned out to be an absolute nightmare to roll with. I figured I had got him wrong as soon as we shook hands, he nearly broke my delicate mitt with a squeeze that King Kong would have been proud of. I pulled guard and decided to put this guy out of his misery quickly with a very fast triangle. Make no mistake the triangle was very tight, but he wasn't for tapping out. In fact, his escape was somewhat unorthodox. He reached for my throat and squeezed. I had to let go, either that or pass out. Holding closed guard was impossible with this fella, his elbows pressed into the inside of my knees and prised them apart as easily as tearing a hole in a wet paper bag. The best way I can describe my 5-minute roll with this bloke, other than pure hell, was grinding, squeezing and absolute torture. It felt like I had been run over by a truck as we ended our 'friendly' roll. I kind of half limped, half dragged myself off the mat not sure whether my bruised and battered body was as injured as my bruised and battered ego. Karl was watching from the side-lines. His grin as I approached said it all, *'I see you have met Jack Mountford then?'* Met him, the guy had tried to kill me. *'Yeah, who is he?'* I weakly asked. Karl told me that he was one of the original Catch-as-catch-can wrestlers and contrary to my earlier assumption that he had foregone badminton to try submission wrestling, he had been training and competing for longer than I had been walking the Earth. In short, I had just been mauled by a legend. It kind of helped to know that my rapidly bruised body and ego were dished out at the (large) hands of a stalwart of our beloved art. Another lesson had been learned, but I am not sure if it is *'don't judge a book by its cover'* or *'don't wrestle with old guys in a young man's sport'*. Either way it was a painful lesson and at the same time an absolute honour to share the mat with Jack Mountford. I still use a couple of the techniques he used that day, and bizarrely at any open mats these days, I'm the guy that the young guns are looking at as Mr Werther's Original.

Catch me if you can - The Gracie Hunter

I have a huge amount of respect for Catch Wrestling. Even before Jack Mountford had illustrated its proficiency on that long summer afternoon in Manchester. I was aware of its heritage in the northern mill and pit towns. Names like Billy Riley, Roy Wood (not the singer) and Karl Gotch were spoken in hushed reverence. Their legacy built on cobbled street and grassy knoll, beneath the shadow of industrial chimney and in the gloom of working-class despair. They forged their skills in makeshift gyms, often no more than a shed with a few mats strewn around. These were tough, no-nonsense people. If they had an issue it was settled in a wrestling bout. The once popular art lost some of its appeal over the years, but never died out completely thanks to the likes of Wood, Billy Robinson and the afore-mentioned Jack Mountford.

There was a healthy rivalry between BJJ and Catch Wrestling and this was to be showcased in spectacular fashion in 1999 when Japanese Catch Wrestling star Kazushi Sakuraba (Sak) faced Royler Gracie at Pride 8. On paper, the clever money would have been on Royler every time, even though Sak outweighed him considerably. Sakuraba had previously beaten Vitor Belfort, a standout from the Carlson Gracie stable and in so doing, put a target on his back within the BJJ community. The fight ended somewhat controversially when Royler was caught in a kimura (the irony of another loss coming as a result of this move at the hands of another Japanese fighter). The Gracie corner objected when the fight was stopped by the referee rather than as a result of Royler tapping out. As hard as the loss was to accept, it set in motion a long and exciting rivalry between Sak and the Gracie family.

Following his win, Sakuraba called out Rickson Gracie. Unfortunately, this was the greatest potential match up that never happened. The timing of the challenge coincided with the death of Rickson's son and understandably led to arguably the greatest fighter in the family re-appraising his life. Rickson retired from professional fighting.

Sakurabu's wins were nothing short of amazing, but as a die-hard Gracie Jiu-Jitsu disciple, I dismissed them as a fluke. Rickson, I reasoned would have easily got the W, and in some spectacular fashion. But, alas, it was never to be.

Chapter 14

Still All White on the Night

'Pulling into Manchestaaaar Piccadilly, where unfortunately there will be a slight delay'

2002-2003

In-between teaching at Alan's gym, I was still making the two-hour round trip to train at Defence Unlimited.

I got a call one night from Karl, *'You coming to the gym tonight?'*

'Wasn't planning on it mate, I am a bit broke'. I replied.

'Oh, that's a shame, I have Royce Gracie teaching at 7.00pm'.

I don't recall where I got the money from, but that night as I waited on the Defence Unlimited mats for the man that was responsible for my addiction, I was just relieved that I had people in my life that would lend me a few quid to realise my dream.

Royce looked just like he did on the dodgy VHS tape that had lit me up a few years before. He didn't smile much and looked as mean as a bag of rattle snakes, in a boyishly handsome kind of way. I was as nervous as hell waiting for the class to start and although Karl had said it was invite only, the room was packed to the rafters.

Accompanying Royce was Marc Walder, who I think at this time was a purple belt. Royce took us through some guard passes and a couple of attacks before telling the eager students to pick a partner and roll. Royce watched as we went at each other like a pack of hungry hippos. Occasionally he would shout at someone to relax and not be so rough (me on a few occasions).

At the call to change partners a rather stocky lad approached me, I had never seen him before and didn't know what kind of experience he had. As it happened, my softly-softly approach wasn't the best idea I had ever had as this lad launched at me with an aggression that a grizzly bear with a very sore head would have been proud of. He smashed me against the beam that stood in the centre of the room so hard that the old building was in danger of collapse. That might have been forgiven had this psycho not proceeded to grind his elbow into my eye socket whilst emitting a rather disturbing growl. Ok, all's fair in love, war, and rolling in front of Royce, I decided. If this idiot wanted to get rough, he was about to get *a can of whoop ass* opened up on him. I used my now tried and trusted scissor sweep, albeit a tad on the hard side. Once mounted I cranked on an 'Americana' so hard that the subsequent crack caught Royce's attention.

'Not so rough' he admonished. I was devastated. This prat had tried to blind me a few seconds earlier and here I was getting told I was too rough by the man that had nearly taken Jason De Lucia's arm back to Brazil as a souvenir from UFC 2.

Time was called and as we all sat around the room, the great Royce Gracie addressed his audience. After telling us how happy he was to be in the UK, he went around the room and occasionally pointed and said, *'you wear blue belt now'*.

It felt a bit odd to me, especially when he gave a blue belt to a bloke sitting next to me that had obviously only done a couple of lessons. If truth be told, I had thought this lad had wandered into the wrong class altogether. I remembered helping him do an arm bar earlier that night, he was so uncoordinated and awkward.

And then Royce's gaze fell on me. He raised his finger and as I held my breath, my heart beating faster than Cozy Powell on speed, he said *'too rough'*, before moving on to award a blue belt to the bloke next to me, Mr Grizzly Bear. I felt devasted. Not by the fact that I was still a white belt, but more for the fact that Royce Gracie thought I was a thug. Too rough. I had dreamt of this moment for so long, and when it finally came, I had let myself get into an ego match and ruined my chances of promotion.

I was also disappointed by the way that the blue belts were given out that night, not that I have a right to question the great Royce Gracie, but I often sit and wonder if somewhere in England there is a 50 something bloke that wandered into a Brazilian jiu-jitsu class by mistake, never to train again, lamenting his grandkids and anyone else that will listen, that he was awarded a blue belt in 'UFC' from Royce Gracie.

Chapter 15

Who's afraid of the Big Bad Wolf!

'The train is about to disembark in Widnes. Please make sure you have all of your personal possessions. Oh, and it's a full moon, so don't go near the moors'

2004

I stayed with Karl and the Defence Unlimited team for a few years. They had aligned with Matt Thornton's Straight Blast Gym (SBG) and I had recently received my blue belt, but something was missing for me. I knew that SBG were/are a great team, but I never really felt a part of it. Maybe it was the fact that I was trying to build my own gym up, or maybe I still wanted to have access to a black belt coach. I had been a white belt in BJJ for the best part of 6 years. Not because I was bad, but because the opportunity to grade only happened at a black belt seminar.

Darren was a blue belt and Karl and Colin Robinson both purple belts at this time as I recall. I became disillusioned somewhat after receiving my blue belt under Matt. After all, he didn't know me from Adam. I hadn't rolled with Matt other than very briefly on the day he gave me my blue belt. I just didn't feel like a blue belt. Which after 6 years seems ridiculous and in today's times of plenty would be, but I hadn't had access to the kind of training that would have warranted confidence in my ability to carry the grade.

I should have been walking on air to receive my blue belt, instead I lost motivation. I stopped going to SBG, I put on a significant amount of weight because I wasn't training properly and was by and large just going through the motions. After all the years of struggle, frustration was weighing me down (not easy with my new fat cat look), but something was about to happen that would turn out to change my life and training from that moment on.

In-between moping about and shovelling large quantities of food into my dial, I was still reading the martial arts magazines. My eyes were drawn away from the fridge one morning by an article about two BJJ black belts that were coming to the UK to teach. This was great news in itself, but the fact that these BJJ brothers were absolute legends and planning to teach out of a new facility in Widnes, was the icing on the cake (mmm, cake). This was the kick up the portly arse I needed.

Widnes was an hour's drive, I decided then and there that I needed to leave SBG and try to join this new academy, The Wolfslair. Back in the day I didn't really know enough about the whole Creonte thing in BJJ, and even if I had, I would have still made the decision to change teams. That's not to say that I didn't agonise over leaving Karl and the SBG team, I did. I am a loyal person and had made some great contacts at the gym, but in the end, we are all given freewill, and mine was to follow my heart and head to Widnes.

Mario and Fredy Sukata

The Sukata brothers had taken the head coaching position at the newly opened Wolfslair Academy. The gym was the brainchild of business partners Lee and Anthony, two diehard MMA fans. Prior to Mario and Fredy arriving in the UK, another BJJ black belt had briefly taught at the facility, but I had never known of his tenure and subsequently didn't train under him.

As it transpired, Fredy didn't stay in the UK, it was too cold for his liking (he moved to Argentina to head up his own school). Mario, the older of the siblings was famous in his native Brazil after taking a bare knuckle, no time limit fight with Dan Severn at very short notice, and at only 21 years old. He had gone the distance with the much more experienced Severn and gained not only the respect of his opponent but also the adoration of the spectators as a result of his resilience and refusal to give up. Severn should have destroyed the young Sukata, who at this time had only had a couple of fights and was so much younger and lighter. It is also worth noting that at the time of the fight, Mario was a purple belt. Mario later attained his black belt under the legendary Carlson Gracie, perhaps the fiercest of all of the Gracie Vale Tudo pioneers and a man who embodied the fighting spirit that Mario displayed in the Severn fight.

It was this 'do or die' approach that Anthony and Lee wanted to foster in their new academy. The academy itself was out of this world. There was, to my knowledge, nothing like it in the UK at this time. It was more in line with some of the American Academies. A large white mat and wall matting led out to a competition sized cage and a boxing ring. It was a sight to behold. In the centre of the mat there was a red circle, which I initially thought was a nod towards the Japanese flag. I later learned that Mario had painted over a Gracie Barra logo. There was a changing room with a sauna and accommodation for visiting fighters and coaches. On floor two there was a viewing mezzanine and kitchen. I had never seen anything like it, being used to sweat and sawdust dives that were cheap to rent. The mats I trained on where usually begged and borrowed old Judo mats that were something of a health hazard due to rips in the cover. They were likely alive with bacteria and how there had been no deaths from Staph I will never know.

Anyway, here I was at the all singing, all dancing Wolfslair. My Gi and new blue belt packed neatly in my training bag, it felt like the first day at school and I was very much the new boy. I approached Mario and after a brief introduction I said that although I was a blue belt, I would have no problems going back to white if that was the result of his appraisal of my skills, or lack thereof. Mario is a really friendly yet frightening looking guy. Standing at over 6ft and adorned in tattoos he has the archetypal image of a bad ass MMA fighter.

That first BJJ session was a real eye opener. There were perhaps 4 students on the mats, 2 blue belts and 2 white belts, and me, a fat, wheezing mess. The first thing that hit you when you walked onto the mats was the cold. It was mid-winter and was in the minus degrees, or at least that's what my rapidly turning blue toes were telling me. Mario sat, or more accurately, huddled atop a gas heater. Plumes of cold breath the only visible sign that he was alive. He wore a hoodie under his Gi and the Brazilian staple of white socks that I had long since given up wearing as tribute to Carley Gracie. In short, he looked freezing and not particularly thrilled.

After a warm-up we got into a couple of techniques. It felt surreal training under the glare, or rather cold hard glare of a bona fide black belt and a Brazilian to boot. Mario had great technique and the session went by in a heartbeat. The time to roll came sooner than I expected. I was apprehensive, anxious even. A heavy feeling in the pit of your stomach, a dryness in the mouth and your heart racing a little faster than is comfortable. It reminded me of the Royce Gracie episode. I just wanted to impress the teacher so bad, to not look like the phoney that I felt. The blue belt tied around my waist suddenly felt like a noose around my neck. There was a lad on the mats that was obviously the mat shark. He was younger than me by quite a few years, bald, athletic and really suited the nickname that he answered to, Kojak. I made a beeline for him as I wanted to see where I was in terms of comparative skill. I quickly found out. I was destroyed in that first roll. He made me look like an absolute beginner. This is it, I thought in between tapping the mat, Mario will remove this blue belt, much like a disgraced sergeant has his stripes ripped off in front of the whole platoon. If Mario had noticed my humiliation, he didn't give anything away. I was breathing so heavily at this point that the cold air I was exhaling must have caused a fog too dense to see through.

I fared better in my next couple of rounds, but the besting that Kojak dished out played on my mind for the rest of the session. I was used to tapping people out, not getting tapped myself. After we bowed out, I decided to take some positive action and asked Mario if he would take me as a private student. We arranged the first session for the following Saturday at 10.00am and off I went into the cold night air to further beat myself up over my dismal debut at the Wolfslair. I felt like the grandma in the fairy story Little Red Riding Hood, that Wolf had torn me to shreds, but what a feeling. Sleep didn't come easy that night as I relived the nights events. I was excited about the one to one with Mario, and at the prospect of rolling with Kojak again.

Chapter 16

Blue is the colour-Jiu-Jitsu is the game

'Staying on track'

Mario had told me not to remove my blue belt. He actually praised my game, which to my self-doubting mind reached my brain as *'you are ok, but man, you have so much to learn'*, which to be fair I knew was the case. Blue belts were thought to have ninja like skills back in the day. I certainly didn't feel like a Ninja, not even close. I felt like an imposter, a Japanese Jujitsu black belt in BJJ clothing. I wanted some kind of magic dust to envelop me when I wore that blue belt, but it didn't.

The way I tried to see it back then, was that BJJ was the absolute antithesis of all of the martial arts training I had done up to that point. But in truth, I was really struggling to let go and walk a new path, to empty my cup, as Bruce Lee had advised. I understood the concept that Lee was alluding to in his iconic statement, I just didn't feel confident enough to throw my Japanese Jujitsu baby out with the bath water, if you will. My cup was overflowing, and I was unable to grasp the idea that I needed to learn afresh. My ego was holding onto that Japanese Jujitsu black belt as if it had it in a death grip. I wasn't allowing myself to identify as Gary the BJJ blue belt. I was still Gary the Japanese Jujitsu black belt because that fed the delicate palate of my ego. If asked what grade I was by someone I had just met, I cited the black belt before adding *'and I have a blue belt in BJJ'*. Don't get me wrong I was proud of my blue belt, I just felt that had that been my only grade, I would have got that pitying look that comes across as *'ah, well keep going, you will get better'*. Which in truth is what I needed to hear.

I might have given up on Japanese Jujitsu, but it wouldn't allow me to move on. A bit like the jealous ex that keeps trying to scupper every new relationship you might pursue since leaving the toxicity of that chapter in your life. I clung to my traditional background like a drowning man holds onto a buoy in a choppy sea; scared that if I let go, I would sink without trace.

As I have matured, I now see the value of coming from a traditional martial art background and I am very proud that I achieved a black belt in Japanese Jujitsu. Anyway, here I was both a black and blue belt, about to enter an environment that might just see me beaten black and blue. But as Del Boy might say, *'he who dares Rodney, he who dares'*.

The jiu-jitsu classes at the Wolfslair were very quiet. I just didn't get it. I had trained with blue belt coaches that had full mats so why, when we had access to someone of Mario's stature, was there only 5 people training, and that was on a busy night. I knew that the day classes for the pro team were busy, but I couldn't wrap my head around the apathy in the evenings. Still, the good thing was that it was almost like getting a private lesson every time you stepped on the mats.

Sometimes some of the other Brazilians that Mario had brought over as part of the pro team would come and train. One night a huge guy with a personality to match stepped onto the mats. Andrew was a purple belt and when you rolled with him you felt the absolute shift in skill between blue and purple. His English at the time wasn't that good but he always made you feel relaxed and at ease when you rolled with him. He didn't look Brazilian; he was more English looking with a paler complexion than Mario and his fellow countrymen. But he was funny, and always up for a laugh, especially when he tried to mimic the Scousers in the class, *'What's up La'* he would say in his best attempt at the Liverpool twang. Mario would belly laugh so hard before saying something to Andrew in Portuguese.

I had been doing 121 sessions with Mario for a few weeks when one Saturday he asked me if I was interested in some MMA training or a bit of No Gi for a change. I didn't mind as any training under Mario was like winning the lottery every single week. Mario called Andrew to come onto the mat and roll with me. We went at each other as we had many times before, only this time I was faring a lot better and at one point caught my new Brazilian friend in a heel hook (on reflection, Andrew in all likelihood gave me the sub). Mario stopped the roll after a while and called me over. He told me that my No Gi game was so much better than my Gi jiu-jitsu. Although disappointed to hear my coach say this, I agreed, but said that it was my goal to turn it around.

We stayed with the Gi after that and a few sessions later, Mario asked me to roll with him. Up to this point I had never rolled with a black belt other than Matt Thornton (and that was 1 roll). I had never seen Mario roll either. This was going to be interesting. Mario lay on his back looking for all the world as if he was chilling after a good lunch. I tried to pass his legs and get to side control but found myself thwarted at every attempt. Eventually he locked guard around my waist, it felt as if my lungs were about to pop. He eased them up, probably as a result of my reddening face and sharp intake of breath. It was obvious that he was playing with me, much like a cat with a mouse just before going for the kill. Every time I felt I was getting somewhere he would make a small adjustment that saw me sailing through the air and onto my back before the inevitable submission. This had the effect of making me go harder. What I now know as spazzing out (not the most politically correct description), that most common white belt trait that we love so much. Elbows were flying in all directions and knees were desperately trying to stay connected to the mat. All to no avail as I was tapping the mat so much, I made Cozy Powell sound slow on the drums.

As time went on, I came to the conclusion that when I rolled with Mario, he had the ability to play his game just above my level. There were one or two times he went all out on me and on those occasions, I quickly learned what it must be like being a plastic bag caught up in a hurricane. Mario probably wasn't even going all out, it just felt that way. I always knew when he was working on a new technique as I would be swept at will or subbed with the move of the day. It didn't matter that I knew it was coming, I just couldn't stop it happening. This was after all, what I had wished for, access to a BJJ black belt so I wasn't complaining.

The one thing that became apparent early on in my training under Mario was the difference in skill sets I was being exposed to. I had rolled with some really good people, but they were a million light-years from being Mario Sukata. The saying *'what doesn't kill you makes you stronger'* was certainly true during these early Wolfslair sessions. It was perhaps my greatest learning curve where I was exposed to such exotic things as the De La Riva guard and X guard. I loved De La Riva guard straight away, but it took me ages to get the X guard to a level that I felt comfortable enough to use it. I would leave those Saturday morning sessions feeling that I would never get the damn thing to work. But I persevered, mainly because Mario wouldn't let me give up. The first time I got an X guard sweep in rolling I felt like I had won the World Championships. Had the current trend amongst anyone winning a medal at a BJJ comp by putting one hand on your heart whilst pointing skywards to the great creator (think Rafa Mendes) been in vogue back then, I might have felt this an appropriate celebration for such an achievement. I would, in all likelihood, also have been hoofed out of the gym by Mario, and rightly so.

In many respects the time I spent at blue belt was arguably my most prolific period. My game changed so much. This was a result of the 121 sessions but also the quality rolling with Kojak and Andrew. The weight was starting to come down too, which was a blessing. As time has gone on, I believe that the blue belt period is when you are a sponge taking in a lot of concepts and techniques that you will, over time, work on slotting into your game, making jiu-jitsu *your jiu-jitsu*. There are things that will fit you and things that won't, but it is a time of empirical research whereby you decide what stays and what goes. As Bruce Lee said, *'keep what is useful, discard the rest'*. Although, in jiu-jitsu, don't just decide that something isn't for you. As an example, had Mario not made me persevere with the X guard, I would have given up on it after a few failed attempts. This is the benefit of having quality instruction and guidance. Your coach is your mentor. They see things in you that you might not.

I had been stuck in a rut prior to training under Mario, I had been a white belt for so long it was hard to change the mentality that I was now a blue belt. And that, I believe, held my progress back. I just didn't believe in myself. It was a long road to blue belt, but now at least I was on the right road. 6 years was a long time to stay a white belt. I imagine that so many aspiring BJJ players dropped out back in the day due to frustration. But there again we still have a massive dropout rate now, in these times of plenty. BJJ isn't easy, whether you are in an academy that is run by a black belt or not. It takes dedication and hard work. Two ethics that can be in their scarcity these days. But it is interesting that the major drop out is seen after people get their blue belts. I had no intention of quitting. I might have had a slight blip whereby I lost my mojo, but I was as determined as ever to keep going. I was totally obsessed with BJJ, it was an addiction. And maybe that addictive gene is the reason that some stick with it. Who knows, had I not found BJJ I might have ended up addicted to a crack pipe, or worse.

BJJ is painful and has led to a lot of my relationships failing. It is hard on any relationship when someone is so blinkered and determined. I was training 6 days a week, sometimes twice a day. I might as well have been in the pub or down an alleyway with a needle sticking out of my arm as far as being a committed and loving partner went. I justified it, just like any addict will, by denying there was a problem. *'At least I'm healthy and learning something of value'* I would protest if challenged. In the end I always chose jiu-jitsu if given an ultimatum, which at some point I always was.

The truth was, just like the addict that drinks to much or gets high, I was always one hit away from self-destruction. You don't think it at the time, but it takes a toll that can affect your everyday life. I personally wouldn't change a thing, but I have to admit that I missed out on a lot of things because of my addiction. And it wasn't just the physical training. I was coming home and opening up books about jiu-jitsu, talking to my friends about jiu-jitsu, eating and sleeping jiu-jitsu. But if we are to achieve our goals, we have to be prepared to make sacrifices. If I wasn't able to make a training session, I became irritable, pacing the floor like a caged animal. I couldn't sleep for thinking that I had somehow failed. I was jealous of my teammates who lived a stone's throw from the gym. I made a two-hour round trip 3 to 4 times a week to train with Sukata, often getting home at 10.00pm, foregoing food and after showering and falling into bed. It's no wonder I was living alone with no mates outside of the gym, my life was all about jiu-jitsu and getting the next fix.

I could never really understand people saying that they only trained jiu-jitsu as a hobby. A hobby to my mind was collecting stamps, train spotting, doing jigsaw puzzles or going to the football on a Saturday afternoon. Jiu-jitsu is a way of life. I reasoned that I was born in the wrong time, I was best suited to times gone by when knights fought for honour and pride. I was, in my head at least, a modern-day Ronin, a samurai without a sword, wandering a lonely path.

I was also becoming something of a martial snob, if it wasn't Brazilian jiu-jitsu, forget it. I would laugh when someone would tell me with pride that their 10-year-old nephew or niece was a black belt in Taekwondo. I resented these fast-food martial arts that promised a shiny new belt every 3 months. The BJJ blue belt was a great achievement, but when you tried to explain that you were a blue belt after some 7 years of training the general reaction from the uninitiated was *'jeez, you must be really crap'*. I did, for a while, try to reason with people but gave up eventually. It was like casting pearls before swine to my blinkered mind's eye. Jiu-jitsu was still an unknown to the vast population who thought that all martial arts were deadly killing systems. Jiu-jitsu wasn't even on their radar. It didn't even come in a close second or third when asked to name a martial art. Karate was king, Judo and Kung Fu the princes in waiting and then there were these *'new kid on the block'* systems like Taekwondo. The general public, in the main wouldn't know the difference between any of these styles, it was all about breaking bricks and taking on five or six thugs with your bare feet.

The Wolfslair, under Mario's coaching, soon started to make a name on the MMA world stage and more top tier athletes joined the roster. It was not an uncommon sight to see Michael Bisping and Quinton Rampage Jackson wandering around the gym, sometimes watching the night-time classes.

These were heady times. The gym's success brought in new students. Those eager to follow in the footsteps of Bisping. Some stayed after the initial enthusiasm flame had died down, most didn't. It was obvious that BJJ and MMA where only for those rare souls that had tenacity and drive. I saw some really talented grapplers come through the doors, but rarely stay beyond a few months.

Over the years I have become more philosophical about these kinds of students. As a coach you invest so much time in their training only to have them disappear into thin air. At first, I would get angry for Mario, he was better than this, how dare these people treat him this way. But as time has gone on, I have mellowed and to a degree, understand this kind of behaviour. Jiu-jitsu is not really for everyone, as the tag line suggests, it is for a select few. That is not to say that even the casual drop in/drop out can't benefit from BJJ. A white belt with a few months training will have a good chance of coming out of a violent confrontation relatively unscathed. What I mean is, to get to black belt takes a certain something that 95% of the population don't possess. I knew that I had it, whatever this 'it' was. The only thing that would force me to quit was death. I believe that I could lose a limb or limbs and still continue in my quest (why has that scene from Monty Python just come to mind).

Anyway, here I was, training under one of the best black belts in the world, a blue belt and an ambitious one at that. I was starting to grow into the grade, maybe I should order that ninja suit now.

Chapter 17

Roll Call

'Feels like a runaway train'

One thing that separates BJJ from other martial arts is its aliveness. This was a term that Matt Thornton coined and something that I have always placed great emphasis on. A lot of martial arts training is about as much use as a chocolate fire guard if it lacks pressure testing.

One thing that we concentrated on, back in the day, (as today) was rolling, the colloquial term for sparring. Mario would start every session with pass the guard, hold the guard, whereby one started in closed guard and had to pass whilst your training partner tried to sweep. You can learn a hundred plus ways of passing the guard, but without practicing with a degree of resistance, all you will have is a set of pretty looking moves. Rolling is jiu-jitsu's forge. The place where you test your metal. Catching a technique that you have drilled in a live roll is the best feeling in the world. But and this is a big but, you have to also spend time drilling. When Mario was teaching me X guard, it at first felt like I would never be able to get it. Maybe I would eventually be able to demonstrate it against a compliant training partner, but making it work in sparring felt out of my reach. This is the magic ingredient for success in BJJ if there is one. It is good to roll, but you have to know the techniques through repetition and drilling, one wouldn't work without the other. I was a blue belt and only just understanding this concept. I loved to roll. And I suspect that most people that start jiu-jitsu enjoy this aspect of the training above all else.

Mario would bellow from atop his gas heater *'Let's roll'* and we would excitedly face our partner, ready to test our jiu-jitsu. Sometimes, and depending on who I was rolling with, my strategy changed. If, for example I was rolling with Kojak I played to my known strengths, the handful of techniques I knew well enough to apply them in a roll. Whilst against someone I knew I could beat; I would try the techniques that I had been working on. It didn't matter in these rolls if my entry to X guard failed and I got caught in side control, because I knew I could escape. But I was, unbeknown to me at the time, a prisoner to BJJ's biggest limiter, the ego. My *play it safe* against Kojak was actually hindering my development.

Squeezing my guard so that he couldn't pass was never going to help me to improve. And besides, he always passed anyway. I should have been opening my guard and trying different options rather than just trying to survive the roll without the humiliation of tapping out. Ego is the dark side of aliveness. On the one hand we are trying to evolve, but the ego is the voice in your head saying, *'don't do that, you will get beaten'*. I believe that ego is the jiu-jitsu equivalent of the Bermuda Triangle, in as much as it has made more white and blue belts disappear than any other factor.

Anyway, I was trying desperately to improve my game. Drilling, rolling and teaching in my own classes. Teaching is also a great way to improve. When teaching a technique, you have to be on point with every detail. Back then a blue belt coach was quite a common sight, nowadays it is unheard of.

But, and I might be shot down in flames for this belief, a blue belt back then was a different beast, we had to be. The grading criteria was, in my opinion, different. As I have stated, I was a white belt for 5 years. I believe that grading and jiu-jitsu have changed as the art has evolved. And although not necessarily true of the majority of BJJ schools, there are some that are less stringent in the deciding factors when it comes to belt promotion. This was to a degree inevitable. It has happened throughout martial arts history. The westernisation of martial arts is heavily influenced by commercialism. We only need look at Karate. In the 1950s and '60s when Karate was first introduced to the western world it was a tough and uncompromising art that was hard to achieve a grade in, let alone become a black belt. The 1970s heralded a golden age in martial arts, thanks in the main to the Bruce Lee movies and subsequent Kung Fu craze.

The demand to learn outstripped supply. In other words, the bona fide masters were hard to find, much like the 1990s and early 2000s when BJJ was in its infancy. This had the effect of a kind of dumbing down of systems, a less strict criteria for grading which soon resulted in more black belts able to meet the demand. That is not to say that this was common practice amongst all Karate black belts. Some refused to compromise, and the art has in the main retained its integrity. The same is true in all martial systems, including BJJ. The main difference is that now we have full time academies that run as businesses. There is nothing wrong in this approach, but it is harder to manage when there are opportunities to franchise, which is when control can be lost and a definite disconnect from the source occurs.

Anyway, without sounding too much like a dinosaur it just seemed different back then. But I suppose it is a bit like every generation talking about *'the good old days'*, things were just different, and that is just the way it is. Evolution is neither a good nor a bad thing, it is just inevitable. Techniques and training methods were different, I recall my first session at the Wolfy, Kojak took the warm-up and demonstrated a series of acrobatic moves that my brain looked at and said, *'no way'*. There was more chance of me pulling Jennifer Aniston than getting my fast-approaching middle-aged body into those contortions. Not that I didn't try, I did, it's just that I couldn't get the movements as easy as the younger lads. I did learn how to cartwheel though, so every cloud and all. Our techniques were what we now refer to as *'old school'*. We didn't know a berimbolo from a paradiddle. We had the De La Riva and the X Guard, and they were our 'exotic'.

The Scientist

Talking of De La Riva, I was lucky to train under him way back when. He was/is a good friend of Mario's and a seminar had been organised at the Wolfy. I hadn't really heard a lot about Ricardo De La Riva prior to this seminar, other than the fact that there was a BJJ guard named after him. Ever the inquisitive student I asked Mario about him one Saturday morning after our usual 121 sessions. Mario spoke eloquently and with admiration for the man he called *'The Scientist'*. *'Is he some kind of inventor then?'* I clumsily asked. Mario explained that De La Riva is perhaps one of the greatest innovators of the modern BJJ game of all time. My interest peaked. I had visions of this mad scientist type; inventing moves in a laboratory type gym in the thick of an Amazonian rain forest, a closed fortress that only the initiated were allowed into the inner sanctum of. A Dr Jekyll meets Frankenstein sort that rarely slept and lived on a diet of coconut water and chickpeas. And whilst my wild imagination might have run amok, the truth was that De La Riva has modified and invented a shed load of techniques that we take for granted. He had also beaten Royler Gracie in one of the biggest jiu-jitsu upsets in BJJ history. The more Mario talked of his former Carlson Gracie teammate, the more I wanted to meet him.

The seminar was held on a weeknight and was not particularly well attended given De La Riva's stature and legacy. De La Riva wasn't anything like my imagination had led me to believe. He was smaller than I imagined and wasn't carrying an ounce of fat on his body. He didn't speak much English, so Mario was translating. Words really weren't needed; this man's jiu-jitsu was on a whole different planet. He showed an arm bar from guard, nothing new, just the five-point armbar that I had learned many years before. But it wasn't the armbar setup that was the wake up and smell the coffee moment, it was the ending. De La Riva showed us that the traditional way was ok but was easy to escape if your opponent stacked you. I knew this to be the case, as I was always getting stacked in this position and subsequently stuck in someone's side control.

De La Riva had a really clever way of stopping the stack that on first look made me wonder how I had never figured it out myself. It was simple yet effective. The solution was that once the armbar is set you immediately hip escape into your opponent, this has the effect of bringing their head closer to the mat and making your hips too heavy to allow the stack. Genius. I was marvelling at this man's analytical brain and affirming all that Mario had told me about the innovations that De La Riva had gifted to the jiu-jitsu world. He might not look like the stereotypical nutty professor, but make no mistake, this man was the real deal.

We then went onto the De La Riva guard, and this again was a real eye opener. I decided that day that this guard was my new favourite thing. The details that *'The Scientist'* shared were game changers and I can honestly say that I still use everything taught that day to great effect.

The seminar was a huge stepping-stone in terms of my development, I really started to analyse jiu-jitsu, pick apart the moves in order to understand the mechanics that make them work. In short, I became something of a lab rat. My aim was simple, to make jiu-jitsu as efficient as possible. In terms of where my jiu-jitsu was at this time, I felt like I had lost a penny and found a million pounds. I can look back on my journey up to this point and see such a huge learning curve. It felt somewhat surreal as if I were Ebenezer Scrooge being visited by the ghosts of the past the present and the future. I had a clarity in my vision, I had learned from the past, I was enjoying the present and the future certainly looked bright.

Chapter 18

Purple Reign

'Moving into first class'

2007-2009

The brightness of my future was hued with a purple glow, I was elated to be awarded my purple belt by Mario. At this time Mario had a grading syllabus. In addition to the techniques required, you were also expected to write about the history of BJJ. I loved this way of deciding if you were competent enough to move onto the next belt. It probably has something to do with my traditional martial arts background. Mario at this time was visiting my academy and teaching once a week. In addition, I was still making the two-hour round trip several times a week and taking 121 sessions.

The UK was beginning to prosper in terms of a BJJ gold rush. More black belts had crossed the pond and a network was being established. There were some great academies dotted around the UK. In Birmingham, Braulio Estima was spreading the gospel having taken over the Gracie Barra Birmingham academy after Mauricio had relocated to London. Chen had moved abroad by this time, and I believe that Mauricio had taken a lot of his old student base. There were, as stated, some absolute powerhouse teams coming to the fore. Carlson Gracie London, Pedro Bessa, Roger Brooking and a host of future movers and shakers. These were healthy and exciting days. The UK was moving into the premier league. We had skulked about in the shadows long enough, now was our time to shout and make ourselves heard.

Purple belt was a very interesting phase in my BJJ life. It is, I believe, one of the most prolific times in the BJJ journey. My game was changing. At blue belt I had developed a really good defensive aspect to my rolling. I could attack, but my emphasis was leaning more towards sweeping and frustrating my opponents. I had to develop a good defence. When you have Mario Sukata passing your guard as easy as a hot knife cuts through butter, you had better be prepared to tuck your elbows in and keep your chin down (I only had the one chin now, having lost some of my pre Wolfy weight gain). It was a necessity to be able to adapt your game.

On one roll you could have Kojak flying around you like a (highly skilled) '*Whirling Dervish*' and then on another there was the size and strength, not to mention the vast talent of Sukata.

The name Sukata is a nickname. It was aptly given due to the pressure that Mario exerts in any control position and came from a car crushing business that was well known in Rio back in the day. So you can imagine that being rolled up by the human equivalent of a car crusher was not a pleasant experience. And if you can't imagine it, take my word, it hurts in a way that I have never felt before.

Mario's brother Fredy also had this gift for applying pressure, I was on the receiving end of it one day when he had come to the UK to teach and visit his brother. The roll started well, I was doing ok, or so Fredy led me to believe. I ended up so tied up that I couldn't even tap out. I felt my spine cracking, my ribs popping and my jaw about to explode under the pressure. The only thing I could do was let out the most pathetic whimper that would have been at home in the whimpering World Championships. Anyway, thankfully Mario heard my pathetic squeak and saved me from a life in a wheelchair and having to communicate like Steven Hawkins.

At purple belt I really started to 'get' jiu-jitsu. The concepts that made sense to me were connectivity and leverage. I knew how to control positions and was really trying to stop using unnecessary strength when applying a submission. My guard play was changing too. As mentioned, I really liked the De La Riva guard and the sweeps that came from it, but I was also starting to develop more of the half guard game. Previously I had seen half guard as a delaying position when my opponent was starting to pass my guard. I wanted to be a good all-round guard player, especially after watching Mario and Fredy rolling. Their skill and flow between positions brought back the memory of seeing Mauricio and Chen rolling a few years earlier. But now, I understood jiu-jitsu better. It was the difference between watching a football match for the first time and then later watching and understanding the offside rule.

The other thing that had changed was the wealth of information that was now readably available. YouTube was establishing itself as the go-to internet site for all things jiu-jitsu (that and cute cats). This was/is a good and a bad thing in my opinion. The good was the access to world class coaches, all willing to offer advice and techniques to anyone that entered the YouTube domain. The bad, was/is, the amount of rubbish that is uploaded by unscrupulous individuals trying to make a name for themselves. One problem was that most people wouldn't know the difference between a good scissor sweep and a bad scissor sweep. The other problem that I have encountered over the years is in the habit of lower belts watching fancy techniques and wanting to learn them before they learn the bread-and-butter techniques such as how to pass the guard, hold positions, apply a simple choke etc. It's the reason you see white belts trying flying armbars and berimbola's in competition, failing and then getting their guard passed and subbed without having an answer to these offensive moves.

YouTube can be used for good or evil I suppose, just like the bible is open to interpretation and misrepresentation. It comes down to what you want or expect from its content. Personally, I would rather train in a 121 and group class than try to learn in front of a screen. Although back in the day I had little choice other than to watch square eyed as the Gracies shared some of their techniques to video. We all learn differently; some need to see, some need to hear and some need to just try. There is no right or wrong way. My preferred way has always been a combination of watching and listening to the explanation of the technique I was being introduced to, this is why I loved both Mario and *The Scientist's* way of teaching. Mario was very hands on, whereas De La Riva explained infinite detail.

It was at purple belt that I started competing again. Previously I had meddled at white belt, but the blue belt years were something of a wilderness period. Mario encouraged his students to compete, and the pre-comp training was brutal. We drilled and rolled extensively anyway, but on the build-up to a competition, the training went up a gear or 3.

The class sizes were building too. I had more hard training in that period than I had ever been exposed to. It wasn't uncommon to crawl off the mats leaving a trail of sweat and the fine mist that forms when hot bodies are subjected to a very cold room.

Mario had told me about the European Championships that were scheduled to take place in Switzerland early in the New Year. This wasn't the IBJJF Europeans but was nevertheless a big competition that would certainly test our metal. There were 4, including Mario, competing and to say that I was excited at both the prospect of competing on foreign soil and watching the great Mario Sukata take to the mats, was something of an understatement. I managed to get a full sponsorship deal for this trip (flight, accommodation and food), so in some respects there was no pressure and in another there was massive pressure. I wanted to win and not just for me but for Mario, the team and the guy that had paid for my trip.

The training had gone well. I felt strong and ready. The day of the flight soon came around and before I knew it, I was en-route to Switzerland to compete in a European BJJ competition. Switzerland is breathtakingly beautiful, and I really enjoyed the long train journey with its panoramic views over meadow and mountain range.

The competition was held in a large sports complex in a picturesque town somewhere in Switzerland. My only knowledge of the Swiss up until my visit was of watches, cheese, leather shorts and steins of beer (or was that the Germans? Apologies to the Swiss if so). The place was rammed and there were a few rapidly gaining a reputation UK BJJ guys in attendance, including Oli Geddes, who at this time was I believe, a purple belt. Oli was a prolific competitor and was a regular on the winner's podium. He trained under Mauricio Gomes' Son, Roger Gracie, another legend in the making. Roger deserves more than just a passing mention. He was destined to become the greatest BJJ competitor of all time, winning multiple World Championships and is undoubtably another nominee for the UK BJJ *Hall of Fame* in terms of his importance in spreading the BJJ word.

Anyway, here I was a nervous wreck of a purple belt, about to walk onto the mats and compete for a European medal for the second time in my life (London 1998 being the first). My first opponent wore a Rickson Gracie Academy patch and hailed from Italy. He was confident, bouncing up and down like a jack-in-the-box, shaking out his arms and rotating his neck. I, on the other hand, stood statue still. My eyes looking deeply into my opponents in an attempt to catch a glimmer of doubt or nerves. There were none. We gripped up and I quickly pulled guard before jumping my legs for a triangle. It wasn't tight enough, so I transitioned to armbar, but he was resisting, even though I could feel his arm popping, I went back to the triangle, and he tapped out. As first bouts go, this was a dream as I had finished the fight early and without tiring. The next two fights went the same way and to my surprise I had won the gold medal.

Mario won his division and also took gold, as did Tony, another of our teammates. Jay got silver but fought really hard, so all in all it had been a great trip. I decided to enter the purple belt *absolute*. I had won gold, so I figured I had nothing to lose.

My name was called first to the mat. There was, what seemed like a very long wait before my opponent was summoned to join me. He was huge and by the sound of his name, of Polish descent. This bloke had muscle on muscle, his arms were wider than my legs (together). He had a short-cropped haircut that made him look a bit like Ivan Drago (*'if he dies, he dies'*). He looked very stern and obviously was taking this a lot more seriously than I was.

Mario, Tony and Jay were on the balcony watching, ready to give good advice should I need it. I looked up and caught Tony's eye. We laughed; this guy was a machine who looked like he intended me serious harm. So, my next move came a bit out of left field. As the very large Polish gentleman turned his back to put on the green and white belt that the ref had given him, I stood on one leg in a Karate Kid pose, arms outstretched in a classic British piss-take. All good so far, the lads were loving my little comedy routine. And then as I looked up at my audience, my Polish friend turned around and saw in full Technicolor my now slightly wobbly one-legged crane. He wasn't best pleased. Although having said that, his face was very still. Maybe he had just overdone the Botox and was finding it hard to smile at my hilarious joke. And maybe not.

The ref started the bout, my Polish friend rushed me and picked me up onto his shoulder before slamming me onto the tatami. I hit the mat so hard that the skeletons of my ancestors rattled. Still, this was a fight, not a flower arranging demonstration. I spun into guard and flung my legs high and caught an armbar. What I hadn't reasoned was how long this guy's arms were, let alone how thick. Mario was shouting *'you have him Gary'*, and that was true for a brief second, my Polish friend had other ideas. He grabbed my Gi at the neck and used his fist to push into my Adam's apple. The armlock obviously wasn't bothering him, whereas his now driving knuckles were in danger of snapping my neck. Something strange started to happen. The sound of the crowd turned into an echo that would have been at home in a large cave, the harsh lighting above me started to dance like a thousand stars twinkling in a night sky, the face of the Polish behemoth contorted, melting like hot wax, his teeth bared and a strange growl emitting from his face, and then it was over. I don't know to this day whether I passed out or the referee took pity and stopped the bout, but it stopped. The lighting and noise around returned to normal and even my Polish friends face seemed a little happier. Still, I had won gold in my division, so all was well with the world.

Chapter 19

Nirvana

'Next stop Rio'

2009

To a Brazilian jiu-jitsu student, travelling to the place where it all started is the ultimate dream. Well, it was for me anyway. Brazil is a complex place, a Third World country that is both beautiful and yet so impoverished. Where the poorest look down from Favela's onto the stunning beachfronts, and the rich and famous rub shoulders with the everyday folk, scratching a living as best they can. Rio has held a fascination with the more discerning traveller since its heyday in the 1920s. Rio is the playground of your favourite matinee idol, where the women are of a beauty that is hard to equal elsewhere on this spinning ball, we call Earth. A statue of Christ casts a long shadow over the locals and offers hope to a sometimes-hopeless existence. We all need something to believe in after all, something that takes us from our reality. The rich cling to the notion that God will recognise their charitable work and change the criteria for a place in heaven before the man with the scythe comes a calling and the poor pray for the riches that they think will bring them peace and freedom from the everyday grind.

I travelled to Rio in 2009 with Mario and Kojak, we were to train and then compete at the international masters and seniors BJJ competition as the culmination of our trip. To an English eye more in tune with Blackpool's *Golden Mile*, my first impression of Rio's expansive coastline was one of wonder and awe. The beauty is indescribable, but I will give it my best shot. The sands are a fine yellow that sweep into the most translucent aqua green waters. Mountain and hilly terrain frame the city and dotted at impossible angles are the Favelas that house the poorest of Rio's locals. On the sea front the beautiful hotels and shopfronts stand in defiance to the obvious paradox of wealth and poverty. The locals are a proud people. Exercising is obviously a way of life to them as you see people running, cycling or working out on the beach gyms every day.

My first night in the city found me in a pensive mood. As I gazed out from the balcony of the 5-star hotel that was to be my home for the next 7 days, I couldn't help but wonder what Rio had been like during the early days of Gracie Jiu-Jitsu. The challenge matches, the rivalries, the beach fights and the building of an empire. The Gracie family were the reason I was in Brazil. It seemed a long time ago that I had first heard of the Gracies and their unique interpretation of jiu-jitsu. I never really thought much about Brazil prior to being exposed to the Gracie Family and Brazilian jiu-jitsu. My limited knowledge was about its carnival and of course had heard the stories about children living on the streets. I had probably seen pictures of *Christ the Redeemer* and I knew about the *Copacabana Hotel* thanks to Barry Manilow. Would I ever have visited Brazil without the jiu-jitsu bug, I doubt it. But here I am some years down the line watching a city come to life as the sun dips into a vast horizon. I wanted a window into the Gracies' kingdom, and I had it.

My mind drifts and I find myself travelling back to 1951 in Rio De Janeiro. Hélio Gracie is standing opposite Masahiko Kimura, his toughest challenge to date. The stadium is packed to capacity, the swell of noise from the crowd is deafening as we wait impatiently for the fight of the century to begin. Kimura is huge in comparison to Hélio, although not in height. The Brazilian is whippet thin, gangly almost. The Japanese master squatted and rooted so firmly to the earth that it would take a tsunami to move him. There is a steely eyed determination in Gracie's eyes. He emits a calm and unwavering confidence that is borne from knowing, just knowing. And then the bout starts.

Kimura and Gracie take grips, dancing around trying to unbalance and turn, unsettle and throw. Feet flick out like antenna, feeling for weakness but finding none. Hands pull, feet follow. Balance is shifted and suddenly Gracie takes flight. The crowd shout, whistle, watch. Gracie remains calm, knowing, just knowing. Kimura senses something. Either victory or defeat, but which of the two evils is not certain. Gracie plays guard like a man that has spent a lifetime playing guard. Kimura works to pass. Hélio sweeps. They roll over and over like two giant crocodiles battling to rule the swamp, locked together, as if one. Japanese Judo in the kingdom of Brazilian jiu-jitsu. Kimura vs Gracie. Each a king of their art, each with as much to lose as gain. And then Kimura latches onto Hélio's arm. The crowd senses the end or is it the beginning? An eerie silence hangs in the air, a stillness all around aside from the combatants. Moving in smaller circles now, the frenzy has all but died. The kill is almost complete and yet the defiance, the never give up, do or die attitude remains.

A crack echoes around the amphitheatre, an arm hangs loosely at a warrior's side, but he refuses to surrender. The bigger of the two, but not in heart, stands. He helps his foe find his feet and the crowd show their appreciation of an epic battle. They each to a man know that they have witnessed history and the birth of a legend. A loss that is a victory. A David vs Goliath encounter that will stay in their memories long enough to pass their lips in wonder to their children and their children's children. Writers will write, poets will rhyme, as painters dip brush to capture in time this story of a home-grown hero. A story I saw all too briefly in my mind.

The fight with Kimura, although on paper a loss, is in my opinion what defines Brazilian jiu-jitsu. It has it all. The smaller, weaker man taking on a champion in his sport. And importantly, Hélio didn't take the fight for money or glory, he wanted to test his art and himself. He knew that he was likely to suffer defeat at the Japanese master's hands. He also knew that the weight and strength advantage would play a significant part in the outcome, and yet he wanted to see if he could survive even briefly against one of the all-time great fighters of a generation.

Kimura was certain that he would defeat Gracie with ease, he had said that if Hélio lasted for 10 minutes he would consider it as a loss on his part. Hélio lasted 13 minutes which might not sound like a victory, especially as the outcome was that Hélio's arm was broken, but it was a pivotal moment in the history of BJJ.

I am not entirely sure why the Hélio vs Kimura fight means so much to me. Perhaps it's that age old adage, *'we all love an underdog'*. It's what makes the Rocky Balboa story so appealing, or our love of people like *Eddie the Eagle*. Those that dare to stand up and be counted. That rare breed of men and women who continually push the boundaries. Defy the critics. Rally against the stereotypes. These men and women show that they are human, not superhuman, just human. They strike a blow for the ordinary and feel very much a part of us. People, like Hélio, defining the saying *'what doesn't kill us, makes us stronger'*.

Hélio Gracie knew that he was building a dynasty. He was already famous in Brazil for his many victories, he didn't need to fight Kimura, but the point is that he *did* have to fight Kimura. Gracie Jiu-Jitsu was his sword and shield, he had to step up. Most of the time society remembers you for your triumphs, it glosses over the losses, the fall from grace. The golden years are what count when history is written. But with Hélio Gracie, the fight that most people remember him for was a loss. It is perhaps fitting that one of Brazilian jiu-jitsu's mantra's is *'there is no losing, only learning'*.

Rio is as magical a place as Narnia or Oz, except the lion's wear Gi's and the wizards invent new sweeps and guards. But the time to click the heels of my red shoes was nearly upon me and I had lots to do and see on this adventure, so I had better wake up and hit the yellow brick road.

The next morning, we took a walk through the streets of Rio. Not the façade-like front that runs parallel to Copacabana beach, but the back streets where you will, if you open your eyes and hearts, see a different side of this city. Children no older than 5 years old lying motionless atop paving stone. Where the hardened local's step over them as they would a discarded rubbish bag. A sad and in some ways confusing sight. Sad because no matter your ignorance or indifference it isn't right, children should be cared for, loved, cherished, not left to fend for themselves with little choice but to turn to crime as a matter of survival. Confusing because this is the 20th Century, there are millions of people that want but are unable to have children. These children could go to a loving home, a safe home. It was clear that Brazil has its problems. There is another side to its obvious beauty that is both ugly and corrupt, arguably like any country in the world we could mention, but that didn't make the sight of these children any easier to accept.

I had heard that some Brazilian jiu-jitsu black belts were working with the children of the Favelas. Giving them training and an alternative to the drug, alcohol and criminality that they might otherwise choose. This is the power of martial arts and community. We can change things for the better.

I wondered if there was a correlation between the harsh living environment and the toughness of the locals. We see it in boxing whereby the best prospects come from the most disadvantaged backgrounds. The *rags to riches* story. It seems true of the Brazilians too. In the early days of the no rules fighting (Vale Tudo), there were no rounds or time limits and little in the way of safety for the fighters, and yet there was a long line ready to step up and fight. These bare-knuckle precursors to MMA were in some respects a way of escaping the poverty trap for some. Not all, as some of the early Vale Tudo athletes fought to prove their styles proficiency, much like the Gracies had done.

Anyway, the back streets of Rio were a shock to say the least. I had to get my head in the game and do what we had travelled halfway around the world to do, train jiu-jitsu. I was after all a guest in this country, I couldn't change a system that was so deeply entrenched, as much as I wish I could.

De La Riva's gym

After wending our way through the back streets, we eventually came to the Equip Gym. The home of Ricardo De La Riva, aka *'The Scientist'*. Once changed we sat on the mats waiting for the great man to arrive. We were the first there so it was a tad nerve racking not quite knowing how many people would show up. I was used to England and its relatively small numbers, so I was surprised when at least 20 people walked onto the mats, and better still they were all black and brown belts with the exception of another purple belt. My mouth must have fell open in shock. I had never seen this many black belts in my life let alone in one room. And then *The Scientist* entered the dojo. I watched in amazement as he went up to every student and shook their hand. He gave Mario a big hug and after a brief conversation in Portuguese was introduced to Kojak and me. He obviously didn't remember us from the UK seminar but that was fine, it was after all a few years ago.

After a brief warm up it was straight into rolling. As we were so close to the competition there were no techniques shown. I paired up with the first of my black belt opponents. I immediately pulled guard. If I was about to be smashed, I wanted to at least give the guy a fight. My opponent stood and I desperately kept my legs locked around his waist. I could sense his frustration and opened quickly and transitioned to an Omoplata sweep. It worked like a charm, my opponent lost balance and rolled with my sweep. I quickly transitioned to side control. I was elated. Here I was in the spiritual home of BJJ, and I had just scored points on a black belt. To put this into context, I had thought that the BJJ in Brazil would be on a completely different level and that even another purple belt or even a blue would be able to defeat me. I had little faith in myself really and this sweep was a huge boost to my confidence. I knew that sometimes black belts would give you something, hell I was used to rolling with Mario and knew that he sometimes let me pass his guard or sweep him, but this was different, I knew that the sweep was legit. The black belt knew it too and immediately went after me. He was desperate to escape my side control. He bucked harder than a wild stallion with a cowboy on its back. I held on. Time was called and I slapped hands with the black belt. He didn't look too pleased, but I couldn't concern myself with that. I was buzzing with excitement and quickly made my way over to another black belt.

Maybe I could repeat my success and maybe not, this guy was all over me like a tramp on chips, I must have tapped out at least 6 times in our 10-minute roll. It was so hot in that gym; I was used to training in a cold industrial unit in Widnes. This was like training in a furnace, I must have lost 7bs in sweat.

After a few more rounds the training session was over. I felt like a God. I replayed over and over the sweep I caught the first black belt with, colouring it and making it brighter in my mind's eye. Kojak had also had some success and was equally as excited. We three all headed for the showers feeling a new confidence. Here we were, two gringos in the land of Brazilian jiu-jitsu, and we had held our own. I realised then and there that it didn't really matter where you trained, it was more about how you trained. We were lucky to have one of the best BJJ coaches in the world teaching us all he knew. But geography wasn't the be all and end all. Yes, in Brazil there were more top-level players, and the training sessions were available throughout the day, but in the end, you have to apply yourself. You can, if you have the right coaching and guidance reach the top, whether you are English, Chinese or from a desert island in the middle of the South Pacific. Hard work and tenacity are what determines your success.

We might have been several years behind the Brazilians, but in that moment, I knew that one day an English World Champion was a very real possibility. The USA had already won on the big stage. BJ Penn and Rafael Lovato Jnr had gone to Brazil and beaten the people that had been dominating the sport for many years. The world was opening up. BJJ was no longer the sole property of this South American country. The western world was snapping at the heels of the Brazilians. And for me, it might sound a trivial thing, but holding my own and getting a sweep against a black belt and a Brazilian into the bargain meant so much to me. I felt like a champion. Now all I needed to do was continue in my quest to move up the ranks in Brazilian jiu-jitsu.

My ultimate goal was as laser like as it had been since that day that I first watched Royce Gracie win the first UFC. I wanted to be a black belt. I knew that the chances of me winning a world title were slim, but that didn't stop me dreaming. And as people often say, dreams can come true, and one of mine was about to be realised in spectacular fashion.

Chapter 20

Brief Encounter

'This feels more like the Orient Express'

They say you should never meet your heroes. I am not exactly sure as to the logic of this, but I deduce that it can often lead to disillusionment and disappointment. I have, over the years, met a couple of people that warranted the title of hero, Renzo Gracie being one, and he certainly didn't disappoint or disillusion me. If anything, I saw him in a different light. I could attach a human element to my idolisation of what can often start as an unrealistic perception of greatness.

Making someone an idol is a way of aspiring to something that we strive to become. In my case, Rickson Gracie was the epitome of everything I wanted to be in jiu-jitsu terms. We often have to accept however that as much as we train, learn or want, we are in all likelihood never going to attain the level of skill of our idols. That is not true of every single person, some will not only attain the level but surpass it. That's just the law of the jungle. There will always be someone coming through that is the next big thing, *the king of the jungle*. I have, as stated earlier, been lucky enough to meet some of the best jiu-jitsu guys in the world, and not only meet but had the privilege of training under.

Martial arts are a breeding ground for heroes. We see our instructors as unbeatable paragons of virtue, wise and all seeing. We can't separate them sometimes from the role and image we have of them, to the everyday living and breathing person that is travelling through life much the same as we are. We all have insecurities, expectations and quirks to our personalities. Putting people on a pedestal is sometimes unfair. In the main, martial arts coaches are decent and humble people that are trying to make a living out of something they love or enjoy. There are however exceptions to the rule. We must beware of false prophets. Those people that build their own pedestal. A pedestal that is often made of nothing more solid than sugar.

Over the years I have seen these cardboard gurus. They espouse home-spun wisdom and fabricate lives that are about as believable as a Hans Christian Anderson fable. Back in the day these paper tigers thought that they were the king of a jungle. They strutted with the swagger of a 1970s disco king. They held court with tales of toughness and fearlessness, and because we only ever saw them in the confine of their jungle (the dojo), we didn't question their sincerity.

When UFC 1 came along, these same fearless martial Demi Gods, had no option but to deride its result. Most of these dojo heroes had never actually been in a fight, let alone a tournament like this. They could see that their bubble was about to be burst in spectacular fashion, and they didn't like it one little bit. UFC 1 was a potential pin that was capable of popping the over inflated balloon that these village hall heroes lived in. Cries of *'my art is too deadly for sport'* became their mantra. The *'they (the Gracies) would never get me on the ground'*, became their stock response to a question about jiu-jitsu. They traded on the mysticism that has filled dojos for decades.

The pull of make believe was greater than the search for truth with most students. They would rather carry on practicing unrealistic techniques against compliant partners that couldn't see past the blinkers that they too were wearing. It is a sad reflection that all of these years later, these charlatans are still making a living by selling a dream that has the potential of turning into a nightmare. Gracie Jiu-Jitsu opened my eyes. It didn't open everyone's, and that's ok. People practice martial arts for all sorts of reasons and there are, in my opinion, no bad systems, only bad instructors.

Thankfully, a lot of the prejudice that BJJ suffered because of these *'Desperate Dan' grade heroes* has now dissipated. Martial artists are becoming more open minded and incorporating ground fighting into their arsenal of techniques, and in turn, BJJ practitioners are cross training in striking arts.

The heroes that we have in BJJ are in the main, tried and tested in combat. There are fewer paper tigers in our BJJ jungle and yet we still see the fake BJJ black belts popping up on YouTube. It is an insult to everyone that has trained under a legitimate coach and gone through the ranking system the hard way. These charlatans are just as bad as the *Desperate Dan* grades of old, out to make a quick buck from a public that doesn't know any better.

We all love those call out videos on YouTube where a self-appointed member of the BJJ police has taken it upon themselves to confront these Walter Mitty types. I cringe as the purple belt cop asks the overweight fake black belt for a roll. The look on the student's faces as their God like mentor squirms and tries to *'get the hell out of Dodge'* unscathed. It rarely ends well.

We often hear that after the dojo bust, the fake has closed their school for a while, but often like a demented jack-in-the-box, they pop up a month or two down the line with a different name and at a new location. I suppose it happens in all martial arts, there will always be a long line of fakes, the type that you meet by chance in a bar, whom within five minutes of the conversation is telling you and anyone that will listen how they once knocked Chuck Norris out for looking at them the wrong way. Or my other favourite, the 30-year-old 12th Dan. It's weird how, once you can get a word in edgeways and tell them that's interesting as you do BJJ, they suddenly remember that they have left the gas oven on, and their granny is home alone.

So, we have established the 3 types of *martial art hero;* the village hall hero, the bar-fly hero and the legitimate martial artist that didn't want or accept that they are a hero to others.

Rickson Gracie was/is the Pele of the jiu-jitsu world for me. From the first moment I heard about him, as stated earlier, he became the epitome of everything I wished I could be in jiu-jitsu terms. He exudes a vibe that is somewhere between samurai warrior and the Dalai Lama.

After I watched the documentary *'Choke'* my fascination peaked. I made it a number one priority on my bucket list to meet this icon one day, I just didn't know how I was going to achieve the goal.

As it turned out, fate intervened. After Mario, Kojak and I left De La Riva's gym that morning we decided that we needed sustenance. Acai was my new favourite thing in the world, I had never tasted something so good, especially after a hard training session, and in the spiritual home of BJJ.

We walked towards Copacabana Beach, each scanning for a restaurant to feed my acai addiction and Mario and Kojak's insatiable appetites. I had never seen people eat so much. These two must have hollow legs. And as if that wasn't bad enough, there wasn't an ounce of fat on either of them. I on the other hand, could gain half a stone from a stick of celery. Life can be so cruel.

As we wended our way through the Rio crowds, my eyes were drawn to a man sitting on a stool at one of the outside kiosks that are common to the city. I laughed and said to Mario, *'hey look at the guy with the Rickson Gracie sweatshirt on'*. Mario and Kojak didn't pay too much attention as seeing someone in Rio wearing something jiu-jitsu related was as common as walking through Liverpool on Match Day and seeing a sea of Everton and Liverpool shirts. As we got closer still, *'He's got the Rickson Gracie baseball cap on too'*, I marvelled. Excited to see my favourite jiu-jitsu practitioner honoured in his home country. Closer still, *'Mario, that is Rickson Gracie?'* We all stopped in our tracks. Mario and Kojak's flip flops suddenly losing the flip to their flop. I picked my jaw from the pavement where it had dropped seconds before and said in as calm a voice as I could muster, *'Why don't we eat there?'*

We approached with the caution of a group of fat American tourists on a safari trip to see the elephants of the Serengeti. I could feel my heart beating wildly against the inner wall of my chest. My legs felt even more jelly like than 20 minutes earlier when I had stepped out of the cold showers at De La Riva's gym. Mario was our leader, so a quick nudge from the pasty-faced gringos saw him face to face with the greatest jiu-jitsu exponent of all time. Some words were exchanged, but as my Portuguese is as fluent as my Klingon, I have no clue what passed between these two BJJ masters.

I recall sizing Rickson up and feeling absolute delight at the fact that he was exactly the same height as me, I had always thought that he was taller, but that might be the stature I had created in my mind of a giant.

Mario must have said something about me and Kojak being huge fans, as Rickson turned to look at our pasty complexions before proffering his hand in the universal (pre COVID-19) display of friendship and greeting. My palm was sweating so bad but how can you refuse the hand of a living God. We posed for a picture and Rickson, if he was pissed off that his lunch was disturbed didn't show it. In fact, he seemed happy to talk to us. I asked him about Kron, and he said that he was training hard and that is why they were in Rio. Mario talked to Rickson about coming to the UK to teach and Kojak offered to pay for his lunch.

What a day. If Carlsberg did the perfect day, then surely this would be it. Not only had I swept a BJJ black belt in Ricardo De La Riva's gym, but here I was eating lunch with Rickson Gracie and in Rio with my coach and training partner. Ok so the sun wasn't shining that day, but you can't have it all.

As we spoke, a homeless man no more than 30 years old approached us. He was asking for money or something, but I couldn't say exactly as I didn't understand. As we were about to give this man a few *reais* (the currency in Brazil), Rickson got up from his stool, walked straight up to the man and after a brief exchange in Portuguese, handed him the rest of his lunch and sent him on his way. I often wonder if that homeless man realises that the lunch he ate that day was served by the great Rickson Gracie.

I started this chapter by quoting the well-known saying *'you should never meet your heroes'*. Well, I can honestly say that meeting Rickson Gracie was in no way a disappointment. Even if it did cross my mind briefly, *'I thought you'd be taller'*.

Chapter 21

Theatre of Dreams

'All aboard the Ghost Train'

Competing in Brazilian jiu-jitsu is exciting wherever it happens, but to compete in Brazil is as magical an experience as you can get. It must be akin to a Karate Ka fighting in Japan, or a Kung Fu student visiting the Shaolin Temple.

The Tijuca Tênis Clube gymnasium in Rio de Janeiro is perhaps the most famous and prestigious venue in the world for Brazilian jiu-jitsu competition. It has witnessed the rise and fall of some of the sport's greatest names. Gracie faced Machado here, Penn took on the Brazilians in their own back yard, and won, and history has been written in the blood and sweat of all that have stepped onto the tatami in this most hallowed of arenas.

There is an atmosphere that is hard to describe. The walk from the train station brings with each footfall a feeling of incomparable excitement and nervousness. A mix of trepidation and pure adrenaline that kickstarts the body and fires up your imagination. As you enter the vast arena, the swell of the crowd hits you harder than a Tyson left hook. The ghosts of the past jockey for position with the excited energy of the very much alive gladiators, here to make their name amongst the elite.

The Tijuca Tênis Clube has witnessed a phenomenal growth in jiu-jitsu. It has given a stage to its past, current and future stars. It is the Wembley Stadium, Royal Albert Hall and Madison Square Garden all rolled up into one creative ball. The jiu-jitsu played out on these mats, in this building, is as spellbinding as any great piece of art or musical composition. It is evolution in motion.

This is where you will see the latest techniques before they are shared with the rest of the world. It is as engaging and exciting as watching a great jazz player like Charlie Parker or Django Reinhardt, you don't know what you are about to hear because they don't know what they are about to play. You only know that whatever it is, it will be incredible, beautiful and have the power to transport your very soul, open up new possibilities and change all that you thought unchangeable.

The Charlie Parkers of the jiu-jitsu world have astounded with their skill and innovative abilities in this venue. This is their showcase, their first night, their time to shine.

This great arena gave birth to legends and the sons and daughters of legends. If you listen hard enough you can hear Hélio Gracie shouting advice to a young Rolls Gracie. If you squint your eyes, you will see Royler Gracie vying for grip supremacy with Mario Sperry. This is the true theatre of dreams, the echo of the past causing a ripple that reaches into the future.

I look down from my bleacher viewpoint. It is a veritable conveyor belt, a who's who in the jiu-jitsu premier league. I feel like a pebble on a vast and endless beach. It is easy to get swept along in this sea of euphoria. You can't help but feel that you are a part of something special, and of course, you are. The time is nearly upon us. This is what we had come to do. Compete on the tatami at this most famous of venues. The training that has gone before, the mental preparation and the personal sacrifices to get here collide in an inevitable way.

Suddenly I am standing opposite my opponent. A rather large American, who had sidled up to me in the bullpen minutes earlier and said, *'You know why they have put the two Gringo's together right?'*. I had no clue, *'erm, no'*.

He went on to explain that the locals really didn't like a Gringo to win, and they hedge their bets by pitting us against each other to minimise the risk of this happening. He may or may not have been right, I had no clue, but he said that he had taken the gold the year before and this was his rationale for his suspicions.

Great, so not only was this American built like a tank, but he was also the defending champion. It's probably fair to point out at this stage of the narrative that I had been moved from my preferred bracket due to there being no other rapidly ageing 82kg purple belts. Go figure.

So here I was in an age bracket below and a weight class above staring into the chest (he was too tall to give the death stare into his eyes) of last year's gold medallist. Oh well, there is nothing gained from whinging.

I am not sure whether it was the magnitude of the occasion, the stage I was performing on or the fact that this dude was just bigger, stronger and better than me, but things didn't quite pan out the way that they had in my head. Damn, I wish *'The Secret'*, had been on my reading list before I decided to do this. The universe, at least on this occasion, was not delivering. I reason, all of these years later, that my American friend, had read *'The Secret'*, and that this was his obvious advantage. The universe was working for him and not, it would appear for me. Anyway, he won, and not only won, but did so in style, so I can't take anything away from him. I had been well trained and felt great prior to this first round defeat so I am not going to make excuses (other than the obvious one about the universe favouring the good old US of A that day).

This may not have been my finest day, but Kojak and Mario saved it from total disaster by winning gold in their respective categories. I was elated to witness my friend and fellow Gringo dominate all of his opponents that day. I thought back to those cold days on the mats at the Wolfslair where we had learned, trained hard and prepared together. This was a great moment for UK BJJ. A Gringo taking it to the Brazilians and winning in style. It still makes the hairs on the back of my neck stand and forces goose bumps through my skin when I remember this moment. Who would have thought that a nation that had no BJJ a few years earlier now had an international champion? I was even more elated when Mario approached Kojak on the podium, and to go with the gold medal, tied a beautiful shiny new brown belt around his waist.

It was then Sukata's time, there was a switch in atmosphere as the elite black belts took to the mats. Mario threw me his stopwatch and gave only one instruction to me *'Let me know how much time is left, often'*.

It sounds like a straightforward job, and it is, but given the magnitude of the occasion I was shaking like a leaf blown in a cold winter gale.

Something changed in the arena, it was as if the atmosphere charged up a thousand levels. The photographer from Gracie Magazine sprinted across the mat and focused his lens on Mario. The arena hushed in reverence and excited anticipation. All around there were matches playing out, but it was as if they had gone out of focus. Mario and his opponent were the only two in the picture.

It was a weird feeling. This was a man I had trained with for several years, and yes, I knew he carried a great reputation, but this was surreal. I felt more nerves jangling for this fight than my own. I need not have worried, Mario had a calmness about him, an absolute belief in his jiu-jitsu. This can only come from years of pushing yourself to the limit, of training in a way that breaks you down before building you back up, stronger and faster than you have ever been.

I had seen some old footage of the Carlson Gracie team. I knew that it was a foundry where metal was tested and forged in the most intense heat. There had been so many great and talented fighters out of Carlson's gym, Mario Sperry, Bustamante, Allen Goes, De La Riva to name drop a few. Sukata exemplified the toughness that the gym was known for. The snarling bulldog logo was a giveaway to the intentions of the Carlson Gracie fighters, they didn't come to make friends, they came to dominate, smash and rip out your very soul. And then, if you were worthy, they would make you their friend, a friend they liked to give a special jiu-jitsu hug to now and again.

I felt sorry for the guy standing opposite Mario Sukata, this was not going to end well for him. And I was right, Mario dominated the bout, he seemed able to move and score as I called out the time as it counted down. He got the takedown, passed the guard, held side control and generally made this man look as helpless as a paper plane caught up in a hurricane. It was a masterclass. The crowd sensed that this was something special, all eyes were on the bout. Young and old marvelled at the display of pure jiu-jitsu that was being served on a golden platter that afternoon. I got so caught up in the carnival-like atmosphere that I forgot the timer in my hand. It mattered not, Sukata was so far ahead on points that only a miracle would change the destiny of this encounter. The time was called on the match, Sukata's hand was raised, and the stadium erupted at the return of the home-grown hero.

Mario's next opponent faired equally as well as his predecessor, he was taken down, passed and for good measure, caught in one of the best arm bars I have ever seen. It was evident that my teacher and friend was on a different level to anyone that day. He was followed on each bout and each mat change by the eager photographer from Gracie Magazine, they knew that what they were watching was something to behold, and so did I.

Mario took gold. It was a great feeling seeing him on the podium, in that most magical of venues.

The rest of the day was something of a fan boys dream. It was something else just to immerse yourself in that arena, with all that talent. There were some real 'A-

list' names in attendance, Mike Fowler and Telles, just to drop a couple. The memory of that day is etched into my mind, a reminder of an occasion that can mean so much.

We came, the three BJJ amigos, to train and compete and that is what we had done. We left, (the two Gringo's at least) with a slightly lobster red colour to our pallor than when we arrived. But we all three were much richer for the experience of training and learning in the spiritual home of BJJ.

We had met Rickson Gracie and spent time on the mats with De La Riva, we had competed in the most famous BJJ stadium in the world, and to a man had eaten our body weight in the local cuisine.

This was my first but not my last trip to Brazil. But it's a bit like your first love, you never really forget, and they always hold a special place in your heart.

Chapter 22

It's All in Your Mind

'The only way to travel'

I am often asked by students, what is the importance of competing in BJJ? My answer never changes. I believe that competition will teach you things that regular classes can't. It is difficult to describe the feeling of stepping onto your first competition mat. The nerves, the adrenal dump, the feeling of being unprepared that first time. It is a massive shock to most white belt competitors when they first compete, they often come off the mat after that first bout absolutely exhausted. They soon discover that it isn't like rolling in the gym, other factors need to be considered. But after they have got that first competition under their belt, they usually know what they need to focus on, be it takedowns, defence or attacks.

There are some students that thrive in competition and show their potential straight away, whilst others never seem to get off the starting blocks in terms of delivering on the comp mat. I have taught some incredible jiu-jitsu ka (practitioners) over the years. People that are monsters on the mat and yet, when they enter a competition, it's like looking at a totally different person. You can often see it in their body language, or they will start to put themselves down prior to that first bout. They have often lost the battle before it begins. That's why it is important to build a strong mind to go with a strong body and game. I saw it in Mario in Rio. That unwavering belief in yourself, but importantly in your jiu-jitsu. Earlier in this chapter I put my own loss down to not being mentally prepared as I hadn't read *'The Secret'*, although a flippant remark, it nevertheless holds some truth, that being, self-belief and the importance of visualisation.

A good friend of mine Alan Levene introduced me to the book *'The Secret'* many summers ago. Alan is a phenomenal boxer and coach, and probably one of the most inspiring and influential people I know. He told me about the book but wouldn't lend me his copy. At first, I thought this to be strange, but looking back I now see why he did this. The book is very powerful and not something you should lend to others. Alan was trying to encourage me to buy my own copy so that I would always have it.

The Secret

So just what is *'The Secret'* and how can it help you in both jiu-jitsu and life in general? There are two, possibly three types of people. Those that are willing to believe that there is a force that is a powerful motivator and creator, those who debunk such notions, and those that don't really give it a thought. I have always been in the middle, neither a believer nor debunker per se, but I have always had an open mind. I am willing to listen, read and research things that I don't understand.

When Alan told me about this great book he had read, I was intrigued. I wanted to know more. Alan told me to visualise something so vividly that I could almost touch it. He said that he had at first been sceptical too, but a simple exercise he uses convinced him that it wasn't just some clever marketing strategy, mumbo jumbo or clap trap bullshit.

He said that the next time I am driving to the gym, I should visualise a parking space being available right outside the door. Our gym at the time was part of a very busy weight-training facility and parking was always a problem. I mulled it over for a while before deciding 'what the hell, I'll give this secret thing a go'.

It was a Thursday night, the busiest of the week at the gym. As I drove I did exactly what Alan had told me to do, I imagined the parking bay at the front of the gym being free. I was concentrating so hard, I almost went into the back of a car, but no problem, I was going to give this my best shot. At least when it didn't work, I could tell Alan that I had tried it, but it wasn't for me. The moment arrived and as I edged around the corner there it was… a full car park, and worse the parking space that had been in my mind, empty, was taken. What a crock of shit I thought as I pulled over to survey my options.

And then it happened, cue the music to the Twilight Zone. The gym doors opened and out came one of the barrel-chested body builders that frequented the establishment, he got into his car, the one that was in the exact place I had visualised, and he reversed out, the space was mine. I edged in, turned the engine off and just sat there. My mind was racing, what the bejesus had just happened. Had Alan fixed it so that I would get the bay? He couldn't have, he didn't know what time I went to set up my classes. Was this asking the universe thingy legit? Is this all it took to get anything you wanted? I couldn't imagine that trying the process to conjure up Jennifer Anniston standing at my door in a raincoat holding a Marks and Sparks meal for two and a bottle of bubbly that night would work, but I sure as hell tried it. She didn't materialise for the record, but I reasoned that it might just be a problem with logistics, she lived in America for a start, that must be it.

Anyway, I was sold on this concept and ordered my copy that night. I read the entire tome in one sitting; it was fascinating. It turns out that all of the great thinkers, the so-called illuminati have practiced the art of positive thinking, asking the universe to provide etcetera. You can't argue with your Leonardo De Vinci's and Einstein's, can you? I got this book somewhere between coming back from Brazil and travelling to Switzerland for the Europeans (the Brazil trip came first but for this book I spoke of the Europeans before the chapter on Brazil).

Anyway, I started to implement the teachings, visualising myself winning gold medals, getting my black belt and yes, I was still hanging onto the Jennifer Anniston request.

Every one of these dreams, if you will, came true. Apart from, you will be surprised to learn, the Jennifer Anniston one. There are some great sayings to inspire us to achieve our goals. One of my go-to sayings is, *'if you can believe it, you can achieve it'*. People like Bruce Lee, who was a prolific reader, believed whole heartedly in the power of the mind. Rickson Gracie also gives this vibe.

As jiu-jitsu evolves, we see a connection between the physical and the spiritual. It is not enough to be strong and powerful, even with great technical ability, if your mind set is wrong or weak you will never reach your full potential. I reason, as I write this, that I always practiced visualisation and asking the universe, way back when jiu-jitsu kimonos were baggy, and it was all seen in black and white, I asked the universe to give me the opportunity to train in BJJ and it delivered. Thanks, Alan Levene, for putting me onto the secret, a secret I am happy to share.

Mind Games

When overseeing a competition class, I try to simulate the actual experience of being in a bout as much as possible. There are a couple of ways of doing this. One method that I use is to put one person in a bad position to start the drill, i.e., side control, mounted, back control etc. The idea is to do a very fast round from this perspective, maybe a two-minute round. But the objective of the drill isn't just to get the person in the bad position to escape, the idea is to say to both participants *'you are down on points; you have two minutes to turn things around'*. By doing this you will get a hard fight for dominance and submission as you don't tell each the point advantage of the other. This will make the students think in terms of going all out right to the end. The bout is not over until the referee stops things, it has an advantage of making the person with control keep working for a submission and the person locked down, fighting until the very end to escape and dominate. There are no winners or losers in this drill it just resets the mind to never accept defeat until it is inevitable.

The best students of jiu-jitsu are those that seek out the hard rolls, the high grades or the nightmare students that give everybody a tough round. They also put as much into drilling and learning new techniques as they roll. Over the years I have seen some really talented people come and go. Sometimes if things come to easily to a student it can signify that although they have an innate talent, they are a touch lazy when it comes to drilling. Alternatively, I see people that try so hard, they want to gain proficiency so bad that they work harder than anyone in the class. They are the ones that you have to politely tell to leave at the end of a session as they would move into the gym if they could.

I was probably in the latter category of students. Although I believe I was born to do martial arts, I have had to work hard to get to the level I have. Back in the day I was frustrated as there were no other BJJ fanatics in my area, so I moved. Then I was frustrated because there were no BJJ black belts, so I waited. When I had the chance to train with Mario Sukata, nothing was going to stop me. I knew that I was the oldest in the class and that I had missed the boat in terms of achieving my goals of fighting professionally in MMA, but it didn't stop me trying. Tenacity is everything when trying to achieve a goal. That and an unwavering self-belief.

It would have been easy to have quit back in the *'olden days'*. I could have coasted along in Japanese Jujitsu, watching my life pass before my eyes, knowing that something was missing but never daring to step away from my comfort zone. There is a great saying, *'if you think you can, or you think you can't, you are right'*. I always (well most of the time anyway) knew that if I just kept going, I would achieve my goal. Life is too short to settle. To go with the flow.

The graveyards are a library filled with stories of broken dreams, unfulfilled lives and unrealised potential. You can hear the echoes of someone at the end of their life saying *'I wish that I had just followed my dream, believed in myself, not listened to the doubters'*. We are only given a short-term tenancy on this planet, what we do with our time is up to us, no one can do it for us. We have to put the time in to get the results. This is where a strong mind is better than any other attribute in helping us in this quest. You can be born to greatness, but without the mindset to keep you moving forward, to realise your potential, all you will ever be is an *also-ran*, a wasted talent, to lie rotting in the next plot to the other wasted talent. People that follow their dreams might come up short to expectation, but at least they have tried, they have dared to dream, and the start of a great endeavour starts as a dream.

My dream might sometimes have felt like a nightmare, but I kept moving forward. I knew from the moment I saw Royce Gracie beating all comers with this funky, alive and kick ass martial art, what I wanted to do. The dream was as vivid as a 3D movie, I could hear each scene in glorious Dolby Stereo. I could smell it, touch it and breath it. I knew I would make it one day; I just didn't know when. And that is the difference between someone that succeeds and someone that gives up, I was never going to stop. I didn't care if I was collecting my state pension when the black belt was tied around my waist, the only thing that would stop this journey was the grim reaper, and he had better come prepared for a fight.

Chapter 23

Walk the line

'Beware, leaves on the track'

2009

I achieved my brown belt in BJJ after I took the gold medal at purple belt in Switzerland, everything seemed to be falling into place. When Mario awarded me the belt, I was overwhelmed. I knew that I was part of a select group of people in the UK, there were perhaps 20 other English born BJJ brown belts at this time. The statistics regarding BJJ were staggering, over 80% of white belts quit, of the 20% that stay 60% quit at blue belt. Brown belts were so rare it was reported that you were more likely to pass a murderer on the streets than a BJJ brown belt (unless the murderer was a BJJ brown belt). At this time there were less than 2000 recognised black belts on planet Earth and only 1.3% that start jiu-jitsu made it to black belt.

The race to be the first UK black belt had already been decided when Jude Samuels, Marc Walder and my nemesis from many years ago, the great Rick Young, where awarded the coveted black belt in Brazilian jiu-jitsu. It was never my goal to be the first over the winning line, this wasn't a race to me, or at least not a sprint. I was a slow and steady plodder, a marathon runner. Not that the first 3 BJJ black belts were in it for the glory of being first either, they had just put their time and effort in a bit earlier than the rest of us. They had travelled to learn, not content with waiting until BJJ landed on UK soil. They were our first men in, the Neil Armstrong's and Buzz Aldrin's of the BJJ Universe, they showed us that it was possible. They were the truly enlightened ones that had discovered BJJ before it was shared with the rest of the world at '*UFC 1: The Beginning*'.

Rick Young came from a diverse martial arts background before getting into Bruce Lee's Jeet Kune Do (JKD). The JKD community after Bruce died was led by his former students, amongst them the legendary Dan Innosanto. Dan was a very forward thinking and innovative man; he had studied martial arts most of his life and was an accomplished Kali practitioner before he met Bruce Lee. It was Innosanto that taught Bruce how to use the nunchaku. Dan was always open to new and revolutionary ideas and when the Gracies and their cousins the Machados set up shop in America, his interest was piqued. Back then, pre-1993, it was much like the UK in terms of BJJ being a scarce commodity. The Gracies were teaching a few people from their garage and planting a seed that not only would grow into a mighty oak but had the capacity to develop into vast forests that spanned the world.

Brown belt heralded a strange time in my jiu-jitsu journey. At white belt and to a degree blue belt, you are very much the nail, always getting hammered into submission by the purple's and above. But white and blue are the most sponge-like in terms of learning this beautiful art. You might be getting beaten on a regular basis, but you are taking in so much.

Purple belt signified to me a depth of understanding that I had hitherto missed up to this point. There was also a bit more pressure on you to come out of every roll with a lower belt at least, on top.

Brown belt felt different again. It was in some respects like attempting to summit Everest, not that I have ever tried it, but in the respect of climbing for days at a time without a view of the top of the mountain. Brown belt was like rounding a corner and catching a first look at the final ascent. You knew that you still had a way to go, but at least you could see where you were headed.

I only competed once at brown belt, I'm not sure why. Maybe I knew that my best performance so far was going to take some beating. Maybe I lacked confidence at this new milestone. The competition I did enter was however, a biggie, the *Paris Open*. I probably, in hindsight entered as a result of never having been to this beautiful city before. Whatever the reason, I don't think my heart was in it and this was reflected in my poor performance. I told myself that my loss was attributed to several factors; I was the oldest in the category, I had had a brutal weight cut, I had only recently been awarded my brown belt and yadda, yadda, yadda, but it was all bullshit. In all honesty, I had lost some of the drive that had been apparent at all the other belt levels, I wasn't putting in the same amount of training or using self-belief to help me get to my goal. The trip to Paris, was in the end, just a bit of a laugh with some good mates. Don't get me wrong, I learned from my defeat, and it gave me a kick up the jacksy, but still it wasn't the bells and whistles affair I wanted at my first outing as a brown belt.

Around this time, my mentor and friend Mario had briefly returned to Brazil. I missed his guidance and teaching, and it showed. I was only really training with my students, who, although very competent, weren't giving me the pressure rolls that I needed to continue to improve. I concentrated more on the science of teaching at brown belt. It was the first time really that I stood in front of my class and didn't feel like a phoney. The brown belt that covered two inches of my waistline gave me a newfound confidence in my teaching ability at least.

I decided, after the Paris match to take a step back from competition and concentrate on building a strong team. I started to look at each technique with a freshness that dared to question the applications. I realised at this belt level that I could add some new ideas that would help to solidify my jiu-jitsu. I felt like Hélio, refining techniques in order to make them fit my game. It didn't occur to me how pretentious I was becoming. *How dare I, a lowly brown belt, think that I could better the techniques set out by the greats that had gone before*. I'm not saying that I actually came up with anything ground-breaking here, I might have, through empirical research found certain nuances, little ways of manipulating situations so that I could gain an advantage here and there. I said earlier that Royce Gracie has stated that his family didn't invent the wheel, but they might have introduced the jack that allowed the wheel to be changed through adding leverage. I hadn't even come up with a basic bicycle repair kit, let alone a jack or a wheel. I also quickly discovered, through the new magic of *'YouTube'*, that my *'discoveries'* had, in the main, already been discovered by someone else. I was in effect, just finding ways to make my life on the mats easier.

Whatever it was, being a brown belt changed my thought process. It is when I started to lose the competitive streak and focus on the teaching side. But it also signified a deeper change in me. Up to brown belt I had viewed BJJ as a really cool way to fight, I mean what's not to love about choking someone out? It is after all a very practical martial art, as demonstrated by Royce and his family, but something started to change in me around this time. I saw that in addition to my art's practical application, a more spiritual connection was coming into my conscious thoughts. I have never been a particularly religious man and prayer is something I have only really tried when the proverbial shit has hit the fan. I am for all intents and purposes, a fair-weather God botherer, a part timer. Someone that doesn't quite believe that there is a big white bearded man (or woman, although maybe without the beard) that sits on a cloud granting wishes and waving a saintly hand that directs us in our daily comings and goings, but at the same time, I am hedging my bets, just in case.

With jiu-jitsu and in particular its merits in the *mind, body and spirit* arena, I was starting to get a special buzz. I could walk onto the mats as low as a snake's belly and leave as light as a helium balloon in a cool breeze. In short, jiu-jitsu was offering more than just a physical high. I started to really get into the *'jiu-jitsu lifestyle'*, a sort of hippy/surfer-like existence whereby you turned your back on the constraints of society. You became a wandering monk like figure, using terms like *'cool'* and *'dude'*. You couldn't have your picture taken without the obligatory thumb and little finger surfer sign (many a wedding photo was ruined as a result).

It was a time of jiu-jitsu against the world, we had a secret that the rest of the world couldn't or wouldn't understand. All of a sudden, the fact that BJJ was an underground movement was *'cool'*. Running a jiu-jitsu class was never about financial gain, how crass? We, the enlightened few, were prophets, evangelists set on a mission to help those that needed to feel the *'spirit within'*.

Our uniform when off of the mats was a hoodie with a jiu-jitsu slogan, a t-shirt with a jiu-jitsu slogan and surf shorts, sometimes with a jiu-jitsu slogan. We adorned our perfectly manicured feet with flip flops resplendent in the Brazilian national colours. You could spot another disciple a mile away. There was a look in their eye, a spring in the step and a ready smile that said, *'hey dude, I'm one of you'*.

We communicated on secret forums where we would debate the meaning of BJJ life and who would win in a fight Rickson Gracie or a silver back Gorilla? These were heady times. We sniggered as our work colleague proudly announced their six-year-old daughter or son had just passed their 1st Dan black belt exam in *bullshitto* or whatever the latest fad in none BJJ arts was that was doing the rounds. *'Wow, 2 years to get a black belt, that's amazeballs'* said with all the sincerity of Donald Trump telling Kim Jong-un that he should get the *Nobel Peace Prize* for his humanitarian work.

It had officially happened, and I hadn't even heard its approach or felt its icy hand on my shoulder, the martial arts bigotry ghost had visited and made me a martial art snob of epic proportions. The usual gym warm-ups were interspersed with some Capoeira, because it looked cool and hailed from our mecca Brazil.

I tried to get that Rickson breathing stuff that he had shown in *Choke* off, but my stomach was more wash basin than wash board and although the ripples looked similar, mine was as a result of the lard that covered any abs that might be lying dormant like underneath.

Yoga was the next fad, it seemed to fit the BJJ lifestyle so well, like coffee compliments cream or Eric Morecambe went with Ernie Wise. How I longed to flop into those cool positions. I wanted at least to get my legs into the Buddha cross legged pose, without the embarrassment of looking like the fat Buddha. My downward dog and warrior one pose were coming along nicely, but try as I might, anything that required a modicum of balance seemed to evade me.

I drew the line of growing a ponytail to go with my new *Boho lifestyle*, I never quite got the fashion on middle-aged men. Likewise wearing my hair in the Jamaican style that seemed on trend was also a no-no.

I also didn't quite commit to the alternative BJJ lifestyle completely. I still worked for the man, as they say, paid my taxes and lived in a comfortable 3 bed semi. I should, by the standards of the BJJ life-stylers been sofa surfing my way around the world, trading BJJ techniques for food and other essentials, whilst broadening my horizons.

I wish I had been a few years younger when UFC 1 ignited my BJJ spark because I think I would have taken to the road and lived the lifestyle to its fullest, but add a mortgage and bills and your options diminish somewhat. Besides, I lived by the sea, I had my own mat space, and I was coming along with some, if not all of the yoga poses. In my head at least I was living the BJJ lifestyle, and my thumb and little finger were making an appearance every time a lens was pointed my way.

I had in some respects come full circle in BJJ fashion, when I started it was all bull dogs and tight lycra with snarling teeth emblazoned on the arse cheeks. My Gi was festooned with patches of other snarling animals, and I was all about the ferociousness of the art. The dojo storming, the rivalry between teams, the code of honour that made *The Godfather* look like your laid-back Uncle Don.

Now it was all about love. We loved and respected each other's viewpoints, we loved the ethos of a BJJ community, we loved sharing our experiences and helping each other. It was akin to the pop culture of the late 70s, when angry young men and women morphed into flower power, nature loving free spirits. It didn't matter that on the mats we still tried to cause each other as much physical discomfort as possible, once the timer had signalled the end of the round it was all peace, love and caring again.

Chapter 24

Black and Blue

'Not the end of the line, just the start of your journey'

2011

In 2011, Mario called me and invited me to a team training session at the Wolfslair. He was due to fly back to Brazil for a while and wanted all of his students there for a big send off session. It was a no brainer really. I had trained with this man for 10 years or so, he had taught me, advised me and supported me every step of my jiu-jitsu journey. I was sad that he was leaving, but he didn't have much choice at the time, so I understood. It was a scary prospect, it felt like we were losing our figure head, our chief instructor and our friend. I wouldn't miss this session for the world.

By this time, the Sukata team had grown. It wasn't a case anymore of 3-4 people on the mats at the Wolfslair, we were a big team that was making waves on the competitive circuit. We had a mix of white, blues and purples on the team, but only me and Kojak held the brown belt grade. I made sure that most of my team were going to be there to give the big man a good send off and was happy with the response that I got.

We arrived at the gym with half an hour to spare, the mat was packed with some familiar and some not so familiar faces. People I had shared the mat with over the years, and people that I would share the mat with in the future. Mario was in a jovial mood, which considering he was going back to Brazil for the foreseeable future was confusing (Mario loves England and wanted to stay).

We got started and after a few techniques, Mario called Kojak and me to the middle of the mats. Apparently, we were to partake in a shark tank. That most delightful of drills whereby you are the fodder for every hungry lower belt in the gym. Something was happening, Mario would never do this unless he was grading someone, and then the penny dropped harder than a Mike Tyson left hook. We were grading, and not just any grade, this was the big one, the black belt.

Time seemed to move in a weird slow motion as one after another of the students tried to tear us a new one. I was holding my own after about 30 minutes, trying to survive and if the odd crafty sub could be taken, I was grabbing it with both sweaty hands. There were some really tough rolls, we were after all a Carlson Gracie lineage team. We didn't fight for point wins; we hunted the submission at all costs.

Like any shark tank there are some easy rolls and some that make you want to die. My next round was against a young man called Charlie McDonald. Charlie was what I would describe as a BJJ natural, he was at the time a blue belt, but he was on a different level and was fit and strong into the bargain. I on the other hand was the wrong side of 40, knackered to the point of dying on those mats that night and hanging on like a cowboy on a *bucking bronco*. In short, I was about to be the main course on Charlie's menu. This was going to be as pleasant as turning up on a blind date to discover Rose West wearing a white carnation. Charlie moved around me like a man possessed by the ghost of Rolls Gracie. My guard was good, but this man cut through it like a knife through hot butter. It wasn't long after that he had me in a kimura. I mustered every last bit of strength I could and managed to bench press my way out of danger, but I knew I was bested, my heart was almost hatching an escape plan through my chest, the only thing missing was the theme tune to *The Great Escape*.

I was relieved when Mario eventually called time, I lay in a pool of sweat, knowing that I had just been to hell and back. I felt lucky to be alive but something else was stirring, an excitement that soon replaced the pain my rapidly aging body was feeling. Was this the moment I had waited so long for, the culmination of countless hours on the mats, the frustrations of yesteryear and the sacrifices made to get to the here and now.

Mario called us to our feet. I was relieved to see that my old friend Kojak was still breathing too, albeit it as hard as I was. It felt like that scene at the end of *Enter the Dragon* when Bruce Lee and John Saxon have survived an onslaught from Hans guards. They wearily make eye contact before giving the thumbs up to say, 'well done, we survived'.

We stood in line, next to those that minutes earlier had tried to decapitate our heads from the rest of our broken and battered bodies. There was, what seemed like, a long ass silence before Mario started to talk. I don't recall much of his speech if truth be told, my legs felt like jelly, and I wasn't convinced they would hold me up much longer. Mario called for Anthony (the Wolfslair owner), who came into the large training room carrying a bag. I heard my name called and moved towards my teacher like a light-junkie- moth to a flame. I was aware that the team were clapping and cheering but it felt surreal. I stood before this great man. A man that had proven BJJ's supremacy in the bare-knuckle arena, a man that had taught me the true meaning of jiu-jitsu and a man that I had been in awe of from the first time I met him. I wouldn't have traded this moment for Rickson Gracie tying that belt around my waist. My brown belt dropped to the mats like a sweat heavy chain, to be replaced by a black belt, that was already heavier in terms of the weight it would place on me. A tear was threatening to break free from my eye, it was wiped away with haste. I was a Sukata black belt, I couldn't show weakness, at least not on this occasion. Mario shook my hand; I turned and babbled some words that as soon as they left my lips were forgotten. I tried to thank those that had been there, Mario of course, my teammates and students, but I forgot to thank the one person that had started this whole adventure, Royce Gracie.

Kojak was next up and was as emotional as I had been at his promotion. I was proud, proud of us both. We had shared these mats for many years, sometimes only accompanied by 1 or 2 others. We had refused to quit, even when injuries made it hard to climb out of bed in the mornings, or in my case, when relationships had faltered as a result of my obsession. And now here we stood as black belts in Brazilian jiu-jitsu. I believe at the time I was about the 30th UK person to be awarded the grade.

It was a bittersweet moment. On the one hand I was as high as a kite caught in a hurricane and on the other, I was sad that my teacher was leaving the UK, perhaps for ever. I also felt the enormous pressure and weight from the shiny new belt that was now tied proudly around my mid-life paunch.

Being a BJJ black belt had been the end goal since I had first seen Royce Gracie dismantling all comers at UFC 1. I had had so many dreams about this moment, that had ranged from the sublime to the ridiculous over the years, and yet now, some 20 years later, I was struggling to wrap my head around this momentous occasion.

I woke the next morning to see the Gi top I had carefully put on a coat hanger and the belt, as black as coal, carefully tied around it. My heart raced and stomach somersaulted as I perused the scene. My phone had been pinging non-stop with messages of congratulations. The Facebook picture of Mario awarding the belt had nearly gone viral, but I still felt like the one schoolboy that hadn't been invited to the popular kid's party. What was wrong with me, I should have been walking around my local ASDA in my Gi and new belt shouting *'Yo Adrian I did it'*. But in reality, I felt as flat as Madonna's voice without the gift of the auto tuner. Of course, I had struggled to accept I was worthy of any previous belt level, from blue to brown, but this felt different again. I felt like an imposter, as if I were on the outside looking in.

Whatever it was, I knew that Mario had awarded the belt because he felt I was capable, that thought kept the doubts away for a while. My first session back on the mats at my own gym felt strange, as if I was overdressed for a party. I was a bit embarrassed if truth be told. In my head I was grappling harder than I had ever done on the tatami. *'How could a kid from the North of England be in this elite bracket?'* It was going to take me a while to accept this.

I started to re-watch those early UFC fights. I marvelled at Royce again. A flame re-ignited and somehow burned as brightly as it had 20 plus years ago. I remembered the conversation I had on email with Royler Gracie and his advice to *'keep going, don't give up hope'*. I looked back on all of the setbacks, as well as the small steps forward, those that had tried to discourage and those that had inspired me to keep putting one foot in front of the other on this long walk.

Then it clicked in my head, I might not be the best BJJ black belt, but I had earned this belt through sheer stubbornness and gritty resolve. The torch had been passed to me and it was my turn to ignite that same flame that had been lit in me many years ago. I might not stand on the winning podium again, but I was capable of sharing my knowledge, coaching and mentoring someone that would. And that was the day I got excited about my black belt, I finally understood that it has the capacity to change people's lives. It is a powerful thing. And as Spiderman says, *'with great power, comes great responsibility'*.

Chapter 25

A Ticket to Ride

'I think I'm gonna be sad, I think it's today'

Yesterday

I have recently gone full-time as a jiu-jitsu coach, teaching for up to 6 hours a day some days. Prior to this life changing decision, I was working 37 hours in a day job that was both stressful and uninspiring. I would leave work at 5.00pm and be in the gym until 9.00pm most days. Something had to give, I was struggling to balance my time. Relationships suffered; I was neglecting those aspects of life that are meaningful. I had a good income, but quality of time was poor. It was a Groundhog Day existence. In my day job all I could think about was jiu-jitsu. My work suffered and I knew that I needed to get away from the 9-5 rat race. Jiu-Jitsu was my calling, and it was calling me to arms, louder than it ever had. I was initially scared of leaving the £43,000 safety net that my day job offered, but the effect it was having on my mental health was too great. I knew that it would be hard to make the change, I was in effect attempting the triple somersault on the trapeze without the safety net for the first time. But after 20 years of juggling the day job with being a martial arts coach, I was ready to make my move.

The decision was made. I would leave my day job and dedicate my time (what little I have left) pursuing my dream to be a full-time martial arts coach. Sounds simple enough, but in practice it was never going to be. I, like many from a working-class background, have been conditioned to live a certain way. That being, to work in a 'normal' (whatever that is) job. Working class, there is a clue in the title. We, the lower echelons of life, are expected to take gainful employment, we are programmed from cradle to grave. Depicted in Dickensian prose as forelock tugging and subservient. From school bell to factory bell, we walk lemming-like towards unfulfilled ambition, missing opportunities that knock along the way. It's not that we don't have the chance to change our destiny, we do, rather it is the shackles of an unseen and unfounded fear should we dare to step out of line that puts the brakes on ambition.

I have always admired those that have swam a course that is against the tide of complacency, those brave souls that took a different path. The actors, the musicians, the entrepreneurs, but I was always only dipping one toe into the choppy waters of river freedom, never daring to dive headfirst into the clear blue flow. I have hedged my bets for 20 plus years, choosing to work and run a part-time business; rather, feeling forced to work. It has been exhausting and hard to focus properly on either endeavour.

Martial arts have been my lifelong love, although at times a cruel and unforgiving mistress. I have dreamed about changing my lot many times, but like many from my class, it was drummed into me from an early age 'not to get ahead of my station'. The graveyards are full of people that 'never got ahead of their station', taking regret to the pearly gates like a letter from your parents excusing you from PE. We will find a myriad of excuses not to step away from the comfort that a regular wage provides. Comfort, that's a joke. What comfort is there in dedicating 40 plus years to an endeavour that makes you anxious every Sunday night as the dark shadow of Monday morning looms ever nearer.

I have always harboured a quiet belief that we are all destined to achieve our worth. Something had directed me to the martial arts, a divine message, a calling. So, at the point that I decided that enough was enough, I went all in. No more hedging my bets, I would either sink or swim, but either way I would be following my dream and sticking a middle finger in the direction of anyone that dared to talk me out of my 'hair brained idea'. You see, people don't like dissention in the ranks, it makes them uncomfortable, and those voices of 'concern', often come from the most unexpected of your circle. They mean well, but they are blinded and shackled by their own social conditioning.

I was lucky that my partner was 100% behind my decision, not once has she poured cold water over my burning enthusiasm. Jiu-jitsu was what I wanted to dedicate my life to. I knew that to be my truth from the moment I saw Royce Gracie being led towards the octagon by his family in that iconic human train. It might have taken longer than I wanted but silencing the voices of doubt that are chattering away in your mind and have been for as long as you can remember, was never going to be easy. Perhaps my greatest victory is the battle to shut out doubt and follow my heart.

My story is far from the light-hearted romp this book portrays, I have struggled with my mental health all of my life (read my first book, *'Karate Doesn't Work in a Phone Box'*, for the warts and all unabridged and very violent version). But Jiu-jitsu gave me more than just physical power, it allowed me to see past the confines that are apparent in a capitalist society, it gave me courage to dare to dream and eventually to follow and live that dream. Jiu-jitsu is so much more than an incredible martial art. It is the absolute dog's bollocks. Little did I know way back in the early nineties, when I saw the first UFC on a dodgy VHS copy, that the impact would be as powerful as any tsunami within me. And the catalyst, a family of Brazilian mavericks, who had also dared to dream would play such an important part in my life.

Chapter 26

End of the Line or New Destination?

'Is it the Flying Scotsman or the bullet train I need to get on?'

This has been one hell of a ride. When I started, jiu-jitsu was in its absolute infancy. It was so new it almost had that new car smell. These were exciting and frustrating times in equal measure. I consider myself to be very lucky in some respects to be a part of the old school, and yet, as I see how far modern jiu-jitsu has travelled, I feel a degree of sadness. It isn't a sadness that is borne from jealousy at the opportunities that today's BJJ students/athletes have, it is more a sadness that as I get older, I am feeling a slight disconnect with the scene. It's not the innovations, the new 'must have' techniques that sadden me, I can do a berimbolo (after a fashion) and try to keep my finger on the pulse of the modern jiu-jitsu game, as much as my rapidly aging body will allow.

What saddens me, is that jiu-jitsu, as I first knew it, is all grown up. It's like seeing your cute child one day marvelling with wide eyed innocence at a digger and the next asking to borrow your razor (even more upsetting if you have a girl).

As an old school BJJ-er I feel like a father figure to the jiu-jitsu community. We nurtured and watched jiu-jitsu in the UK go from shy child, turn into a petulant teenager and finally emerge as a confident adult. When I say I feel disconnected, it is a bit like listening to your 18-year-old sons' taste in music. It all sounds a bit out of sync to my old ears and I can't dance to its rhythm. We all think that the music of our generation was the best anyway. Every age talks about the good old days, but jiu-jitsu doesn't belong to any generation, it is not the property of anyone or anywhere.

The Gracie family were/are, if we are sticking with the train analogy, the Robert Louis Stevenson of the jiu-jitsu world. Stevenson's steam train was a great and useful invention that improved people's lives beyond imagination. It opened up the world to those that until its invention, had little or no chance of broadening their lives with travel, to see that there is a big old world at their disposal. Fast forward to today's modern incarnation of the train. It bears little resemblance to the slow, but strong old steamers of Stevenson's day. And whilst the new trains are faster and offer more comfort, there will always be those that prefer the feel, the smell and the experience that only the old steam train can afford. Jiu-jitsu is just like that, the old school jiu-jitsu that Hélio and Carlos developed offered the same benefits of that first steam train. It has improved people's lives and given opportunities that previously hadn't existed. It is ever moving and opened up a new world to many.

Never has there been a better time to travel and train, share knowledge and grow the jiu-jitsu community. Whatever direction the wind blows jiu-jitsu in, I will be sailing with it. I am too invested to stop. I don't think I could even if I wanted to. My body is only functioning because of jiu-jitsu. Unlike a lot of other combat arts, jiu-jitsu fosters longevity. You can train, if you are smart, into the autumn of your life. As I get older, I think that I am becoming wiser in my training, but then you are on the mat rolling with some ambitious 20-year-old and something switches in your head, you go into another mindset where age doesn't exist anymore. And I don't particularly think it is an ego driven state, I think it is more to do with a survival instinct, a will to win.

The saying *'there is life in the old dog yet'*, seems apt and I am grateful that I still have some life left in me and the teeth to bite if needed. But it is true that you have to adapt your game as time goes on, you are no longer capable of long periods of scrambles. You have to impose a different game plan, to frustrate and slow the action, to make the person you are rolling against make that one mistake that you can capitalise on. It really is a game of inches.

I recall hearing young gun world champions talk about rolling with Hélio Gracie when the grandmaster was well into his 80s. To a man they would say that although he didn't tap them, they in turn couldn't tap him out. Maybe jiu-jitsu in later life is about survival rather than winning. Having said that, I have always rolled to finish a fight with a submission, maybe that will change as I go into my 60th, 70th and hopefully 80th summer. If I am still on the mat then, let alone still breathing, I will be a happy man. It will be interesting to see which train I get off, the old school, the new school, or the new old school.

Chapter 27

Standing on the Shoulders of Giants

'A Brave new world'

I think back to that day that the Gracie family entered my consciousness. Goosebumps rise on my skin, my heart beats a little faster, I am filled with an excitement that is hard to define, yet still apparent all of these years later. In biblical terms, my 'awakening' was like Moses receiving the ten commandments. I knew the moment that I saw that first UFC tape what I was meant to do. We are all, I believe, put on this earth for a reason. The real tragedy of life is that some people never find their purpose, or if they do, they get so bogged down with societal expectations that they give up on their dream. For some, a 'calling' is something that you are unable or unwilling to ignore. You might try, as I had for many years, to juggle the day-to-day expectation and the dream, but eventually something has to give, and you realise that it is an almost impossible task to try and become the best version of yourself in this way. Our true self is within us all, but like a block of clay has to be chiselled away to reveal the true beauty of the sculpture, we too have to lose the excess weight that we carry (not physically), the parts we play to fit in, the image we try to portray, so that we are not found out. We hide our true selves beneath these layers, it is this that we must chip away in order to reveal our truth.

Thomas Edison, the inventor of the electric lightbulb gave praise to those that had gone before when he said that he was standing on the shoulders of giants. Martial arts are no different. Without our forefathers we wouldn't be rolling about on a variety of soft floor options, trying to choke the bejesus out of a mortgage advisor called Richard or a scaffolder called Mick.

Edison knew that without the discovery of fire and later gaslight, his quest to light up the world would be an infinitely more difficult task. Not impossible, just harder. We all need a point of reference. The caveman that rubbed two sticks together to make fire took inspiration from the sun. The man that discovered that pulling on the teats of a cow would harvest milk took his inspiration from… God knows where. But the point is, it started with imagination. Imagination so great that it changed the world.

Whilst Edison gave us the power to light up the world, Hélio Gracie and his family gave us the power to light up <u>our</u> world.

As I write this, I am feeling an absolute freedom. As if the chains that have bound me for so long have fallen from my body. My days consist of teaching jiu-Jitsu, MMA and writing. My creative aspirations are realised, and I am able to live my authentic life, a true gift. It's no matter that I may only have a limited shelf life before I meet Hélio at the pearly gate of the dojo in the sky, I am happy. Happy that I got on the Gracie train many years ago, and happier still that I am still traveling, marvelling at all that unfolds from this first-class window seat.

Thank you, Hélio, Carlos, Royce, Rorian, Rickson, Renzo, Rolls, Carlson, Mario and Fredy Sukata, my students past and present and finally, every last one that has made this trip so special. OSS.

Gary Savage 2021.

Epilogue

Run Over by a Train

This Morning

I wake from a deep slumber, my eyes struggle to adjust to the light that is squeezing through the tiniest of gap in the curtains. I stretch, my body aches in places that I don't even know the medical term for. Every inch of me is sore. My 57-year-old body is screaming out for the soothing feeling that only a hot bath, foaming with a herbal muscle relaxant can provide. I know that as soon as I get out of the healing water, I will be good to go, at least for another day, but first have to navigate the stairs. God, I hate the stairs, especially first thing in the morning. Each step feels like the final ascent to conquer Mount Everest (I imagine, as I've never actually climbed Everest). My posture makes Quasimodo look like a fine and upright citizen.

My progress from bed to bathroom is slow, it has to be. I doubt that if the house caught fire now, that I would get out safely. This is my reality. My body is a train wreck. The result of a guilty night of pleasure, rolling about the tatami like a latter-day Peter Pan, tying myself and my opponents into knots. I know at the time that I will pay for my *Devil May Care* attitude. I convince myself time and again that tomorrow will be different, that I will awake fresh and glowing with good health, but deep down I know that I won't, so why do I continue? What makes me want to put myself through this daily torture? It's simple really, I am an addict. Jiu-jitsu is that first taste of vodka to an alcoholic, the hit that a mind-altering substance gives the junkie, the roll of a dice that excites the gambler every time they bet, because this time they are going to win big. My addiction is as fierce as anyone's, I need a hit every day. And just as the alcohol and drugs take a toll on the misuser, my particular vice of choice leaves my body in a state of disrepair, at least for a while.

After my morning walk to the bathroom, a stretch and sometimes an anti-inflammatory breakfast, I am raring to go again. I have trained so long that I don't, in all honesty, think my body would hold up if I quit. The knots in my back and shoulders are holding me together, the creaking of my knees, fingers and shoulders are somewhat reassuring, at least they still do what they are supposed to do. In short, I can live with the aches and pains. The benefits that jiu-jitsu provides outweighs any physical pain. I tell myself this so many times it becomes a mantra rather than a statement.

I wouldn't change anything (well maybe a couple of things). We are lucky if we are able to look ourselves in the mirror without shame, regret or reproach. Real tragedy isn't found in death, it is found in living an unfulfilled life. Thanks to jiu-jitsu my life has meaning.

And then my phone rings.

'Hello.'

'Yeah mate I want to come and train at your gym.'

'Ok what is it you want to do, BJJ or MMA?'

'I want to fight.'

'I repeat, what do you want to learn, have you done any of these arts before?'

'No.'

'So, you need to learn the art properly in a beginner session.'

'No Fam, I'm a fighter, I just haven't had a go in da cage or stuff.'

(Sighs.) 'So, when you say you are a fighter, have you boxed or trained in another combat art?'

'I am a street fighter. I've had fights and I can handle myself so I won't need no beginner's session Fam, can you get me a fight?'

(Sighs.) 'Ah ok, I didn't realise, my bad, why didn't you say that sooner?'

'When can I get a fight. My mate said he rang you about UFC but you don't do that so what can you get me on?'

'Why don't you come down Tuesday night, that's when we do the UFC class. The team will be happy to have someone of your credentials on the mats. Bring your mate too.'

'Sweet, see ya then Fam.'

'You certainly will Fam'.

I know I'm going to burn in hell, but if several decades in pursuit of BJJ excellence has taught me anything, it is not to take life too seriously. Thanks for reading. Fam.

If you have enjoyed this book, check out other titles by the author.

'Karate Doesn't Work in a Phone Box'. Available on Amazon.

www.garyjamessavage.co.uk

Printed in Great Britain
by Amazon